Read Assure

Guaranteed Formula for Reading Success with Phonics

by

Everett Ofori, MBA, MSF

Read Assure: Guaranteed Formula for Reading Success with Phonics

10-digit ISBN: 1-894221-05-2
13-digit ISBN: 978-1-894221-05-4

Second Edition

Illustrations: Ahn Soo Kyoung

Enquiries concerning reproduction outside the scope of the above should be sent to:
Everett Ofori
c/o Takarazuka University of Art and Design Tokyo Campus Building 1F-123MBE
7-11-1 Nishi-Shinjuku
Shinjuku-ku
Tokyo, Japan 160-0023

Dedicated with gratitude to my brother,
Chief Stephen Abraham.

Other Books by Everett Ofori

1	*Prepare for Greatness: How to Make Your Success Inevitable* © 2013 – ISBN 10: 0921143001 ISBN 13: 978-0921143000
2	*Succeeding From the Margins of Canadian Society: A Strategic Resource for New Immigrants, Refugees and International Students* Written by Francis Adu-Febiri and Everett Ofori © 2009 – ISBN 978-1-926585-27-7
3	*Guaranteed Formula for Writing Success* © 2016 ISBN 13 978-1-926918-22-8
4	*The Changing Japanese Woman: From Yamatonadeshiko to YamatonadeGucci* © 2013 – ISBN 10: 1894221044 ISBN 13: 978-1894221047
5	*The Global Student's Companion:* *10,001 Timeless Themes & Topics for Dialogue, Discussion & Debate Practice* Compiled by Everett Ofori © 2015 – ISBN 10: 1-894221-02-8 ISBN 13: 978-1-894221-02-3
6	*Guaranteed Formula for Effective Business Writing* © 2011 – ISBN 978-1894221108
7	*English Language Mastermind: From Confident Communication to Higher Test Scores* © 2018 ISBN 10: 1894221168 ISBN 13: 978-1894221160
8	*Guaranteed Formula for Public Speaking Success* © 2018 ISBN 10: 1894221079 ISBN 13: 978-1894221078
9	*3,570 Real-world English Phrases for Speaking & Writing Practice, Volume 1* © 2018 ISBN 10: 1894221125 ISBN 13: 978-1894221122
10	*3,570 Real-world English Phrases for Speaking & Writing Practice, Volume 2* © 2018 ISBN 10: 1894221133 ISBN 13: 978-1894221139

Acknowledgments

Much gratitude to Ms. Yuko Bernard, of Bernard English School, Japan, for giving me the opportunity to share my phonics ideas with young learners at the Bernard schools (Ibaraki).

The success of this program is evident from the numerous young people, who through this program, have found joy in reading and are therefore able to approach their study of English with something akin to ecstasy.

Many thanks also go to Mr. Frank Pridgen, Manager of Bernard English Schools, who has been a champion of phonics instruction and has provided invaluable comments to improve this book. In addition, all the teachers who have wholeheartedly adopted this book for use in their classes deserve commendation and their experiences and comments regarding how to make this book more useful to their young charges will always be welcome.

Finally, any errors or omissions in this book remain solely the responsibility of the author.

Sincerely,

Everett Ofori

Note to Teachers, Parents, and other Reading Coaches

Why phonics?

Phonics allows new readers to link sounds with letters. Children as young as four can be taught to read using phonics. When taught right, the parent or instructor will be pleasantly surprised at how quickly a child can catch on to reading in English. Many children's books in English contain very difficult words: *Rumpelstiltskin* by the Brothers Grimm; Mr. Fitzwarren in *Dick Whittington*; Brobdingnag in Jonathan Swift's *Gulliver's Travels*. You will be amazed that once children have acquired the rudiments of phonics they can manage to read, sometimes with just a little help, such difficult looking words.

Children have no difficulty at all understanding the concept of linking each letter with a particular sound. It is but a short leap for them to extend this knowledge from short two and three letter combinations such as "ba" and "na" to "banana" or "can" and "did" to form "candid."

It is also liberating for a kid to understand, for example, that ***fan*** is made up of three sound units: /f/ /a/ /n/. Soon enough there will be exceptions for the child to learn but these exceptions will be welcomed by any child who is continuing to mature mentally and thus is able to grasp subtleties and challenges to previously-learned conventions! Children, even as young as four and five, based on my experience of teaching children that young, possess the capacity to understand that, in some cases, two letters instead of one represent a sound unit. For example, in the case of **short**, /sh/ represents one sound unit while /or/ represents another sound unit and /t/ represents yet another sound unit.

High frequency words

There are a number of words that appear so frequently in English that learners need to know them as soon as possible. These words can also be taught through phonics, but they are so important that they should be drilled into the minds of learners both through repetition and phonics. Some of these words are presented below.

High frequency words that need to be drilled into learners through frequent exposure, including spelling, reading, writing, and phonics.

The	It	Who
This	It's	What
That	Him	Where
These	Her	Which
Those	She	When
There	He	Why
Then	Are	Whose
	Were	While
	You	
	Your	
	Was	
	How	

One method that has been found effective is to list a group of high-frequency words on a board and have the learner repeat after the instructor. When the learner encounters any difficulty the phonics elements are sounded out by the reading coach. The words should not always be presented in the same order otherwise the learner will not really learn to recognize them but simply rely on memory, making it difficult to read them when these words are encountered in other settings. When a learner has difficulty with "WHO" for example, break it down as follows: /wh/ /o/ and sound them out separately for the learner to follow. Likewise, with "WHICH" one might sound out /wh/ /i/ /ch/.

Pronunciation note: To / Do /Me

In the subsequent pages: **To** and **to** are words in their own right and should be pronounced as follows: The girl is going **to** school.
To- (with the hyphen), however, indicates that this sound unit might be connected to another sound unit. Read as in: Toronto. Thus, **do** as in **Do** it for me; but **do-** as in **Do**nut. **Me** as in Give it to **me**. But **me**- as in **Me**mo**.**

Spelling Convention

This book uses American spelling convention, so you will see "color" instead of "colour" and "favor" instead of "favour." This is simply for the purpose of consistency and does not reflect preference of one convention over the other. Reading coaches, instructors, and parents would do well to expose children to reading materials from different English-speaking worlds and to make children aware of these subtle differences.

Read Assure - Methodology

Some words or syllables are presented first in a table format (in rows and columns).

First, the instructor reads the items on the top row, one at a time. After sounding out each item, the student is asked to repeat it. The instructor and the student go through all the syllables or words in the top row and then proceed to follow the same pattern in subsequent rows.

If the instructor senses that the pronunciation of certain words or syllables by the student was not good enough, it would be a good idea to focus on those particular words and sound them out, with the student repeating after the instructor. Once the instructor is certain that the student fully grasps the pronunciation of the phonemes, words or word units in a table, the instructor points at the "words," or sentences below the table, one word at a time, and gives the student an opportunity to read them out. When the learner makes a mistake, the instructor asks the learner to try again. If the learner is unable to do so, the instructor sounds out the problem word or unit and the learner repeats.

The text below the tables uses as many words from the table as possible and also may use words that have been covered in the past.

It is important for the instructor to review previously covered material from time to time in order to ensure that these remain fresh in the mind of the learner.

For Adults

Adults who did not have the benefit of phonics training and feel a need to improve the flow of their reading can equally benefit from *Read Assure*.

Drill Book, Not Story Book

An important point to keep in mind is that *Read Assure* is a drill book, not a story book. The goal is to build fluency from the use of this book and to get children reading picture books, story books, and eventually novels and other works.

In the first few pages, thanks to the illustrations, learners can catch some of the meaning. Instructors might also explain the meaning when asked but the focus should be on the drill. The element of meaning can be emphasized when reading other works such as story books.

Part of the challenge, for children, is to equip them to read far beyond what might be expected and thus make their acquaintance with reading at their own level so much more comfortable and appealing.

Instructors who agonize that the children cannot understand everything they read are apt to give up, thus foregoing the potential benefits to be gained from building the necessary fluency in the learner.

When a learner acquires fluency first, subsequent learning experiences can focus on other aspects and be so much more meaningful and fun.

Three steps forward, one step back

To ensure that learners have the benefit of continual review, the instructor or parent may, for example, cover pages 22, 23, and 24 on the first day. **This is done after first reviewing the alphabet, both capital and small letters, over and over again until the learner has mastered them.**

On the second day, instead of continuing from page 25, you start at page 23 (or even page 21). The learner, therefore, has an opportunity to review some of what was covered in the past. Let's say, on the second day, you cover pages 23, 24, and 25. On the third day, instead of continuing from page 26, you start at page 24, thereby, allowing the learner to revisit some of what had been covered before. **In the first 100 pages or so, it is a good idea to always review the alphabet (pages 17-21) and the two-letter words (pages 22-24) before starting the lesson for the day.** It may seem irksome at times to review what the learner already knows but in my experience many children continue to confuse certain letters long after they have passed their sixth, seventh, eighth, ninth, or even tenth birthdays. It is amazing how quickly some children forget these combinations. Keeping these two-letter combinations perpetually in front of the learner, therefore helps to etch them permanently into their minds and to aid them in sounding out longer words. Doing two or three pages at a time is perfectly all right. As the reading becomes more difficult there are times when the learner will be content to focus on only one page. More ambitious learners, however, will find no difficulty doing four, five, or even six pages at a time, in which case the instructor should avoid overexerting the learner.

If only a few pages are covered at a time phonics will continue to be seen as fun. If the instructor tries to push the learner too hard, then it can become a chore. A wise instructor will therefore find the balance between continually extending the boundaries of knowledge for the student and knowing when the student is too worn out to benefit from the learning exercise.

There are some children, however, who find genuine joy in pushing themselves. Such ones should not be denied.

The value of repetition

If after going over the material on a page several times, the student still finds it difficult, make a note of that page and return to the same page the next time around rather than moving on to the next page. In some cases, you might have to revisit the same material or page two or three times before it sinks in for a particular student. This is perfectly normal as different students have different abilities.

Dyslexia or genuine confusion?

The need to review the alphabet continually is important. Children often confuse their b's with their d's and their p's with their q's. In some countries, there is no faster way for a kid to become labeled as dyslexic than to pronounce a "b" as a "d" or a "p" as a "q." These letters are similar and if the student has not paid particular attention to them, they can be very easily confused. As you give learners the opportunity to review these confusing pairs over and over, they will begin to get them right and all without the necessity of branding them as dyslexic for life! This is not to say that dyslexia is not a possibility, merely that children should not be written off so quickly just because of what might be genuine confusion of elements that clearly look alike.

Building Fluency: Ramping Up

By page 150, learners should have grasped the basic concept and be doing a marvelous job of reading. The overall flow, in general, may be too choppy as learners focus too much on sounding individual words rather than reading in chunks. Instructors or parents ought to model reading from page 150 with an emphasis on how words flow into one another and request that learners read after that fashion. This will lead to a distinct improvement in the overall flow and quality of the learner's efforts. This should be kept up, with frequent reminders when it seems that the learner has lapsed into the habit of sounding out individual words rather than focusing on clusters of words.

Text size and white space

In the first 200 pages or so, a large font is used. This is no accident. The large size and white space make the text less intimidating for beginning readers. As the book progresses and the learner's reading ability improves, smaller and smaller fonts are used.

g or g; a or a

In this book, **g** and **a** are predominantly used. These forms predominate in written works while **g** and **a** are mostly used when people write by hand. In my own experience, it does not pose much of a problem for children when **g** and **a** are introduced to them as easier ways to write **g** and **a.**

Supplementary activity: Using the Whiteboard

Draw a table on a board and break down words in syllables, for example, CA NA DA.
For very young learners, have them repeat after you first the letters (C-A) and the sound (ka).

Thus:
C-A [ka]   N-A [na]   D-A [da]
At this point pause and ask them to read out the word: CANADA
You may demonstrate this process a few times until they catch on. Here's a sample:

Ca	**na**	**da**		**Pa**	**na**	**ma**		**Ba**	**na**	**na**		**Ma**	**Li**			
An	**go**	**la**		**Ba**	**li**		**Ma**	**ma**		**Pa**	**pa**		**Ca**	**ta**	**li**	**na**
Co	**ca**	**Co**	**la**		**Mo**	**na**	**co**		**Fan**	**ta**		**So**	**Go**			
Mo	**na**		**Li**	**sa**		**Ala**	**ba**	**ma**		**O**	**ki**	**na**	**Wa**			
Yo	**ko**	**ha**	**ma**		**Shi**	**na**	**ga**	**wa**		**Bo**	**lo**		**So**	**lo**		

The table below is simply to assure instructors that children have all the sound units they need in this book to become confident readers.

Sound unit samples/phonemes in *Read Assure*

Sound unit	..as in	Notes	*Page*
A	any		79
A	am		22
E	he		22
E	let		39
ee	fee		74
Ii	bite		89
Ii	bit		61
O	go		22
Oo	not		40
oo	good		66
Uu	mum		58
Uu	union		241
Bb	bat		48
Bb	debts	Silent 'b'	134
Cc	circle		222
Cc	catty		41
Dd	dog		50
Dd	handsome	Silent 'd'	139
Ff	fat		48

Sound unit	..as in	Notes	*Page*
Gg	ginger		149
Gg	gap		63
Gg	gnome	Silent ‘g’	135
Hh	hot		69
Hh	honor	Silent ‘h’	115
Jj	jam		48
Kk	keep		84
Ll	lam		48
Ll	palm	Silent ‘l’	103
Mm	man		36
Mm	mnemonic	Silent ‘m’	164
Nn	no		22
Nn	autumn	Silent ‘n’	163
Pp	papa		26
Pp	psalm	Silent p	134
Qq	queen		115
Rr	rat		48
Ss	so		22
Ss	aisle	Silent ‘s’	166
Tt	table		81
Tt	castle	Silent ‘t’	136
Vv	van		62
Ww	won		38
Ww	answer	Silent ‘w’	54
Xx	box		188
Yy	royal		55
Zz	zany		55
bl	table		81
cl	clone		87
fl	flow		154
gr	grass		89
sn	snake		148
tw	two		83
st	stool		179

Sound unit	..as in	Notes	*Page*
sp	spring		118
ch	chick		174
ph	photo		167
sh	she		39
th	think		98
th	than		184
th	asthma	Silent 'th'	190
wh	who		42
um	umbrella		123
un	uncle		152
ow	cow		56
ow	blow		155
oy	boy		55
oi	oil		70
ng	sing		88
ai	bail		85
kn	knee	Silent k	103
ge	germ		222
ge	get		66
on	con		63
-one	bone		87
-one	gone		87
wr	wrong		164
-it	fit		48
-ite	bite		89
-mp	chimp		106
ed	bed		74
-ly	only		41
-ing	wing		113
gl	glad		83
fr	from		72
ay	may		80
sm	smart		81
-ack	smack		100

Sound unit	..as in	Notes	*Page*
-eck	neck		137
-ick	pick		101
-en	eaten		153
en-	end		67
-er	over		69
ea	eat		39
oa	boat		85
ch	chef	Ch pronounced as 'sh'	141
ch	chop		106
ar	art		55
ou	coup		134
ou	bout		173
or	honor		115
-ow	blow		155
-ow	cow		56
-own	known		86
-own	brown		89

The above has been provided to assure instructors and parents that this book has all that is necessary to help a beginning reader master as many sounds and words as possible.

In reality, however, the table above need not form a major part of the instructor's use of this book in helping the new learner. What is required is the instructor's own confidence in his or her reading ability and pronunciation. This is why a native English speaker or someone of near-native ability will be much better equipped to help the new reader than someone who never learned to master English reading.

Why many non-native speakers still cannot speak English well: one theory

In many non-English speaking countries, it is not uncommon to hear people lamenting that even though they have been studying English for many years they still cannot speak English. For some of these individuals, it is a matter of great consternation that after making so much effort fluency in English still remains elusive. Upon closer questioning, however, one finds out that even after so many years of apparent study these individuals cannot sound out many English words confidently. Their reading may be choppy, and they may linger over many words unsure of how to sound them out. Because they never learned to read with ease they may never have formed the habit of reading English books. Often, these frustrated learners will say that they know a lot about grammar but studying grammar books is not the same as making reading a habit.

It is only the individual who has learned to read fluently and with ease who is likely to find reading a pleasure. Learning to read fluently will not mean that one automatically has a free pass into English comprehension. The reader, however, who makes the dictionary a constant companion while also making reading a habit will soon find a whole new world to explore.

In many cases, the beginning reader will be able to infer meanings from the context and sometimes from accompanying illustrations. Those who make reading a habit, however, will, in time, become fully attuned to the flow and music of the language and will, without much mental exertion, be able to reproduce sentences that follow the conventions of English even if their knowledge of grammar is minimal.

A person who reads a lot but has no opportunities to speak with native speakers may be worried that he or she is not progressing. When such an individual truly makes reading a habit, it will come as a pleasant surprise that when opportunities for communicating arise, the floodgates will open and all the years spent in making the mind fertile with vocabulary, syntax, and semantics, will pay off in effective communication.

When one learns to read English *fluently* and makes reading a *habit* it will be almost impossible not to be able to speak English when one is thrust into an arena where opportunities for active communication exist.

The English Alphabet

Capital Letters

A	B	C	D	E
F	G	H	I	J
K	L	M	N	O
P	Q	R	S	T
U	V	W	X	Y
Z				

The English Alphabet

Small Letters

a	b	c	d	e
f	g	h	i	j
k	l	m	n	o
p	q	r	s	t
u	v	w	x	y
z				

The English Alphabet

Capital and Small Letters

Aa	Bb	Cc	Dd	Ee
Ff	G g*	Hh	Ii	Jj
Kk	Ll	Mm	Nn	Oo
Pp	Qq	Rr	Ss	Tt
Uu	Vv	Ww	Xx	Yy
Zz				

***g** is often the preferred form when writing by hand

Show me….

L	E	Q	V	D
B	R	F	Q	M
Y	K	C	W	G
H	S	X	C	N
T	A	J	D	P
I	Z	P	U	O

Show me….

p	c	l	u	m
h	f	s	z	x
o	y	e	h	n
i	a	c	g	j
r	f	q	t	v
b	w	r	k	d

Two-letter combinations

So	Go	Lo	No	To
Do	Be	He	Me	We
Of	On	Ox	Or	Oh
Ab-	At	As	Am	Al
Ag-	An	Ah	Ad	Af-
In	Is	It	If	Ba
Ga	Sa	Pa	Ma	Na
Ha	La	Wa-	Va-	Ya
Up	Us	Ug-	Um-	Un-
Wo-	Zo-	Mo	Bo	Yo
so	go	lo	no	to

do	be	he	me	we
of	on	ox	or	oh
ab-	at	as	am	al
ag-	an	ah	ad	af-
in	is	it	if	ba
ga	sa	pa	ma	na
ha	la	wa-	va-	ya
up	us	ug-	um-	un-
wo-	zo-	mo	bo	yo

My	By	Ma	Ba	Sa
my	by	ma	ba	sa
Yu	Yo	Im-	ma	ko
He	Be	We	Me	Wa-
Ca-	Ja-	Ma	Ba	Sa
Li-	Ni-	Na-	No	Fo
Si-	Ga	Go	Ri-	So
Ji-	Ra-	Ar-	Or	No
Pi-	*Bi-	Da-	Ka-	Bo
Wo-	Yi	Yo	Ye-	Ro

***Introduce "Bi" to readers as in "bin" or "bit". Later on, they can learn other forms such as "binary."**

So Go **so go**

Sogo

Lo Go lo go

Logo

So Lo so lo

Solo

Mama
My Mama
My Mama is at Sogo.

Papa
My Papa
He is my Papa.
My Papa is at Lala.

Ha ha ha!

Ho ho ho!

So	Lo	He	Ba	Is
so	lo	he	ba	is

He is solo.

Baba is solo.

At	An	As	Am	Al
at	an	as	am	-al
Mo-	To-	Pa	pa	-mo's

I am Nolo.

I am Lomo's papa.

Up	Go	So	My	By
up	go	so	my	by

He is up. I am up.

Oh my! He is in Sogo.

He	Is	On	An	Na
he	is	on	an	na

An na Anna

Anna is my mama.

Nolo is on. Baba is in. I am in.

I am in Sogo.

Nolo is in Sogo.

Go	No	On	To	Onto
So	Lo	On	An	Na
so	lo	on	an	na
Da	Dada	Wa-	Wawa	Ka

Go on or go in?

Dada Sasa Bata

In or on?

Go	It	He	Is	Up
Ba	Bar	On	The	The

Go up!

Go up on the bar.

He	Is	On	An	Na
Ox	Of	Od-	Odd	Off

No!

Is it my ox? It is my ox.

Is it in? It is in.

Pa	Na	Ma	Sa	La
Go	He	It	Is	In

Sasa is in Panama.

Am	Al	As	An	Av-
Ma	La	Sa	Na	Va-
a-	Al-	as	an	av-
ma	la	sa	na	va-

Mama Papa

It is Alma.

A-	Up	Us	My	By
So	Go	Lo	No	To

Nolo is in Sogo.

I	Am	am	So	so
Go	go	We	we	Ba
Lo	go	Bo	no	Bono

I am Sogologo.

Sogologo is up!

Sogologo is in.

La	Na	Pa	Ma	Ga-
la	na	pa	ma	ga
On	Of	Or	Me	Us
Ra-	Wa-	Va-	**Sha-**	**Cha-**

Lala

Sogologo or me?

It is us.

Pa	Na	Ma	Ra	Sa
pa	na	ma	ra	sa

Ra ma Rama

Sa sa Sasa

Na pa Napa

Pa pa Papa

Ma ma Mama

I am

We are in Panama.

In	Is	It	If	Ra-
Na	Pa	Mi	to	ra-

If we go, I am in.

We go to Nara.
We go to Napa.
We go to Panama.

In	Is	It	If	Go
in	is	it	if	go
I	so	we	he	am

I am in if we go.

We do so.

We do go.

It is he.

I am he.

At	Ad	As	Am	Al
A	Ad	an	If	Go
ma	Man	ha	has	Map

Adam

Aman

A man.

A map.

Go to Aman.

Adam, Al and I go to Aman.

A man, Adam, is in Aman.

<u>Can you write</u>?

Banana

Panama

Mama

Papa

Sasa

Baba

Lala

Sogo

***Can you write*?**

Bono

Logo

I am Sogologo.

I am Gologoso.

Bolo

Dodo

Mako

Yo-yo

Toyota

Totoro

Momotaro

Let	Us	Go	Up	And
Wi-	-th	with	Sh-	She
Eat	Meat	seat	heat	feat
Sha-	Sho-	Shi-	Shy	Sh-

Let us go up and eat.

Let us eat meat on the seat in the heat.

It is a feat.

Let go of me!

No letup.

Fa-	Ti-	Ma	Ko-	Yu-
fa-	-ti	ma	-ko	-yu

Fatima

Yuko

Mako

Go, Mako, go!

Yu-	Ko-	ba	ra	ki
Iba-	ko	ra	go	ma
No	Not	Us	bus	But
To	To-*	to	-to*	Mito

- To-*As in **To**ronto
- -to* As in Lot**to**

Yuko is in Ibaraki.

She is in Mito, not Miho.

Ku-	Ma-	Si-	Ti-	Fa-
Her	His	this	That	the
On-	And	-ly	With	Abby
At	Fa	Fatty	Catty	Natty

Fatima is in Kumasi.

Her mama is in Miho.

Her mama and papa? No, only her mama.

And Andy? He is with Abby.

Ro-	To-	Wa-	Ko-	-ro
Is	In	It	If	No

Is Mom in Ibaraki?

No, she is in Panama.

Ki-	Ta-	Wa-	No-	not

Is Dad in the Bahamas?

No, he is not.

Wh-	Who	What	My
Why	Whose	By	Why

Who is he?

He is Sogologo's pal.

-en	-ich	-ere	My
Wh-	Who	What	Why
When	Which	Where	Whose

Wh-	-er-	-ere	Where
Wh-	-i-	ch	Which

Where is he?

He is in Aoyama.

Yu-	Ko-	Ka-	Ki-	Ke-

Yuko, Yuki, or Yuka?

It is not Yuko.

It is not Yuki.

It is not Yuka.

It is Takako.

Where is Takako?

She is in Minami Koiwa.

O my!

Tu-	To-	Ta-	Ti-	Te-
Mu-	Mo-	Ma-	Mi-	Me-
Pu-	Po-	Pa-	Pi-	Pe-
-kyo	Ka-	Na-	Ga-	Wa-
Ch-	Sh-	Chi-	Shi-	Shin
Chi-	Cha-	Shi-	Sha-	Sho-

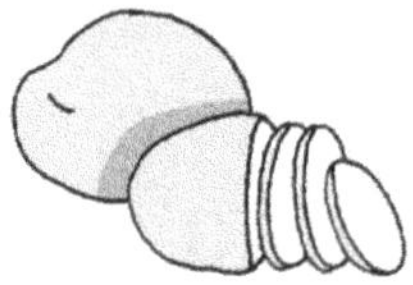

Potato

Tomato

Can you read? Can you write?

Tama

Mama

Pepita

Papa

Tata

To-ron-to

Mimi

Pepsi

Cat

Coca Cola

Tokyo

Kyoto

Kanagawa

Chiba

Toronto

<u>Can you read? Can you write</u>?

Chiba

Shinagawa

Alabama

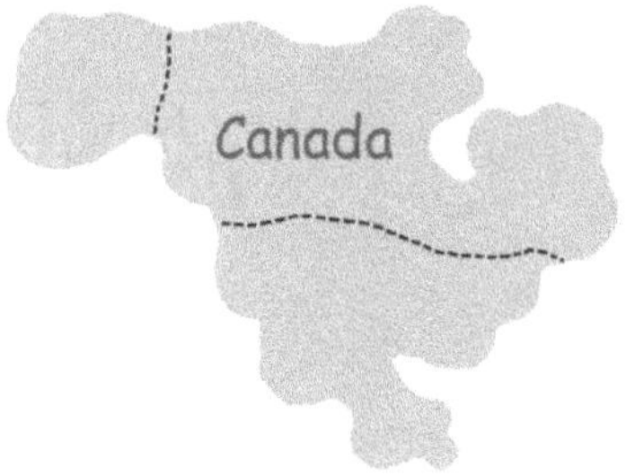

Canada

Okinawa

Shibuya

Mito

Miho

Ami

Kanagawa

Tokyo

Kyoto

Nara

Nagoya

Can you read? Can you write?

Koiwa

Shinkoiwa

Taiwan

Congo

Alabama

Canada

Toyota

Kawasaki

Kalahari

Sahara

Bahamas

Mali

Togo

Tanzania

Zambia

Aloha

3-letter combinations+

Bat	Cat	Fat	Sat
Rat	Mat	Vat	Hat
Fan	Tan	Can	Wan
Jam	Lam	Sam	Dam
Lip	Dip	Sip	Nip
Sit	Zip	Fit	Wit
Has	The	Are	She
Run	Sun	Bun	Pun
Pan	Pat	Pal	Pad
Mad	Map	Pot	Pompom
Pod	iPod	iPad	Put
Tap	Tad	Tar	Rat
Ram	Lab	Wad	Rag
Den	Pen	Yen	Ken
Paw	Jaw	Law	Saw
Bonbon	Zap	Zit	Nil

A fat cat.

A fat cat sat on a rat.

A bat in a vat.

A cat.

A bat.

A rat.

Who	What	When	Where
Which	Whose	How	Now

Where is the rat?

In the bag.

And	The	She	Cat
Dog	Bog	Log	Fog

A fat cat and a dog are in a bog.

A dog in a fog?

Sit	Log	Sat	Mat

Sit on the mat.

He sat on the mat.

Jam	Lam	Sam	Dam

A man can jam.

Sit	And	Fit	Wit

He is fit.

He has wit.

He is fit and has wit.

The man on the lam is mad.

Ma-	Am	Is	No
Mad	Madam	Man	Map

Is madam mad? No, madam is not mad.

Wo-	Man	wo-	man
With	Da-	Dad	her

A woman can jam.

A woman can jam with her dad.

A gal can jam.

Lip	Dip	Sip	Nip

Dip and sip.

Go and sit up.

Go	Sit	Log	Fog

Go sit on the log.

Go and sit on the log in the fog.

So	Go	Lo	No	To
Togo	Sogo	Soda	Copa	Cabana

Sogo Logo

Solo Soda

Sogologo is solo in Sogo. He is not in Togo.

Bat	Mat	Fit	Not

Bat bat

Man man

The man has a bat for a pal.

A bat.

A bat is on the mat.

The bat on the mat is not fit.

We are fit.

We sit on a mat.

Win	Sin	Din	Won
I	We	He	You
Who	Why	When	Where

I win.

He won.

Win	Sin	Din	Won

Din is a sin.

He won.

He won and I won.

Win	Son	The	Won

The son won.

Ox	Box	Fox	An
Are	Ant	Art	Amp

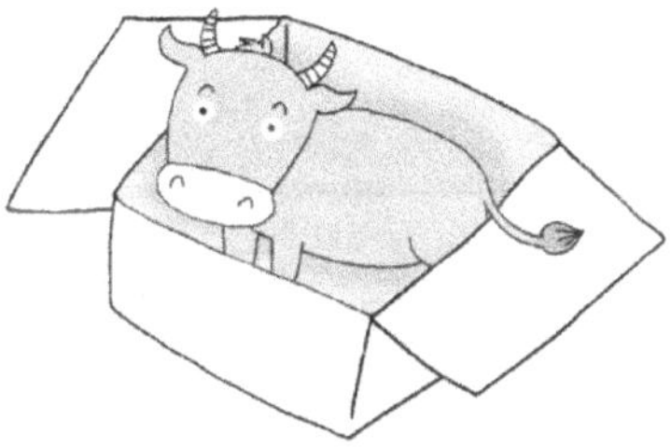

An ox in a box!

A fox and an ox are in a box.

-oy	Boy	Coy	Soy
-al	Royal	Loyal	Alloy
Gal	Lon	Gallon	London

The boy is coy.

The fox is coy.

The ox in the box is coy.

Roy is so loyal. He is a royal to boot.

The boy is loyal to his mom and dad.

Cow	Bow	Wow	Now
ill	Will	Till	Sill
Who	When	Which	How
Bus	But	Cut	Hut

The cowboy is ill, but he will bow.

Now?

Wow!

Jam	Lam	Sam	Zip
Vim	With	But	Cut

I can jam.

Sam can jam.

Sam and I can jam.

So	Go	Lo	No	Won

Sogo has a logo.

I won solo.

It is a solo logo.

Has	Jam	Lip	His

He has jam on his lip.

Fit	Log	Sat	Mat
-ing	Al-	Ba	Ma
Are	He	She	Ship

A fit dog sat on the log.

A fat rat is on the mat.

We are in Alabama.

A bat and a rat are in a jam.

Fit	Sit	Jig	Jog
Mom	Mum	Rum	Mud

He is not fit to do the jig.

He is not fit to go to Sogo.

He is going to Alabama with his dad.

I am going to Miho and Mito with my mom.

His mom is mum.

Win	With	Won	Kith
Run	Sun	Bun	Pun
Yes	Les	Bes-	Wes-
She	Shy	Sham	Shot

Run run

Sun sun

In the sun he can run.

She can run on a bun.

She can pun. She is in the mud with a bun.

Oh no!

She	Shy	Sham	Shot
Les	Lest	Bes-	Best
Nest	Test	Fest	West

Yes. Les, Bes, and Wes are in the sun with a bun.

It is the best test in the west.

The fest is fun.

run	sun	bun	pun
gun	dun	fun	She

She can run and pun.

Sam is on a log in the sun.

Ate	Ale	Bun	Ill
Ask	Bask	Mask	Cask
Eat	eat	Heat	Feat
Bit	Hit	Kit	Sit

I eat a bun.

Sam can eat a bun.

She had too much soda. She is ill.

Sam ate a bun; he is ill.

Why did he eat a bad bun?

Do not ask me. Don’t ask me.

Sam has a mask. He put on the mask and ate a bun.

Did	Lid	Kid	Rid
Now	Wow	Cow	Bow
Log	Can	Dog	Sip

Sam can eat a bun on a log.

Dan can eat a bun on a log in the sun in a fog.

Wow!

He is on the lam.

For	Can	Dog	Sip
Did	Rid	Sid	Kid

The kid did go to the cow.

Rid the kid of the can and the lid.

Sit in the van and sip.

Ban	Bam	Bar	Bad
Car	Cap	Mad	Map
Cut	Cup	Cud	Run
Con	Cop	Cod	Com-
Din	Dim	Dip	Dis-
Dub	Lub	Cub	Sub
Gal	Gap	Gab	Ran
Gum	Rum	Sum	Sun
Too	Loo	Coo	Woo
Soon	Look	Cook	Wood
Will	Till	Hill	Pill

The conman has a cod.
He is going into the loo.

The gal ran into the woods.
She will go into the hills.

Bun	Gum	Sum	Run
She	Shy	Shut	Shun

She has gum.

She can gab with the cook and look at the sun.

Ban	Bam	Bar	Bad
Up	Up	Un-	-der
Under	under	amber	Samba

A bad cat is in the barn.

The barn is amber.

A bad car is next to the barn.

A man and a cat are in the barn.

Car	Cap	Cad	Cut
Has	Had	Ham	Hat
The	There	This	That

There's a man in a cap!

He is a cad.

He has a bad cut.

Con	Cop	Cod	Far
Who	Why	When	Which
Eat	eating	The	are

He is a cop. She is a cop. It is a cop.

The con and the cop are in the bar.

The con and the cop are eating cod.

The cop's cap is on the car.

Why is the cap on the car?

Too	Loo	Coo	Boo
Car	Bar	Far	Dim
Cop	Hop	Lob	Sob

The barn is dim.

The cop is in the car.

Cup	Rum	Sum	Cat

The cat has a cup.

The rat is in the barn with a cup of cola.

Oh my! Get it out of there!

Th-	The	They	Then
This	That	These	Those
There	Food	Wood	Mood
For	Form	Fort	Ford
eat	Meat	Beat	-ing

The rat is eating; it is in a good mood.

This is good.

Ben	Den	Ken	Hen
Pen	Chen	Wen	Yen
End	Mend	Send	Wend

That is a hen with a pen.

The pen is not bad.

The hen is cool. It has a pen.

Boo	Coo	Loo	Too
Book	Cool	Look	Took
The	They	Then	This

They are cool.

They look good.

The books look cool.

Boom	Coop	Loom	Toon
cook	look	nook	good

The cook looks good.

The cook and the books look good.

Th-	The	They	Then
This	That	These	Those
There	Food	Wood	Mood
For	Form	Fort	Ford

Is that food for them?

Did they come out of the woods?

Those look good.

These look bad.

For	Form	Fort	Ford
Force	Horse	Morse	Norse

That pig is in a Ford.
There! Look!

-er	Over	Ever	Never
Not	Got	Hot	Pot

Look over there.
Never! I will not look!

Cap	Bad	Fan	Man
Jug	Mug	Oil	Boil
Join	Joint	Joins	Joined
Her	His	Arm	Elbow

A bad fan dips his hat in a jug of oil.
Is it a man?

No, look! It is not a man. It is a woman.
It is Anna Maria.
She has a mug in her hand.
It is a big, red mug.

You	Cod	Gum	Gap
This	That	These	Those

This is not a car.

It is a cap.

We are not in a car; we are in a big cap.

You	Cod	Gum	Gap
Oil	Boil	Coil	Soil
Hot	Pot	Dot	Cot
Sip	Lip	Hip	Rip

You are in.
I am on.
You are in and I am on.

He boils the oil. He puts the oil in a pot. It is a hot pot. He sips the oil from a cup with dots on it.

Who	What	Why	When
Where	Which	Whose	Gum
How	Wow	Bow	Gown
Ill	Hill	Pill	Mill
Know	Knew	Known	Knock
She	Wish	Ship	Chip

The gal has gum. Wow!

She is in a gown.

She bows in the gown.

It is a red gown.

Who is she?

Whose bag is on her arm?

-ee	Fee	feet	feel
Sh-	Sheet	leek	Geek
Tee	Teeth	-er	Teeter
Ch-	Cheek	It	Chit

She has a chit. She has her fee.

She has a sheet of paper. She has her feet on the sheet. She is a geek. She has her teeth in a leek.

edge	hedge	ledge	wedge
piece	since	rinse	wince

The geek is at the edge of the bed.

She teeters at the edge of the bed.

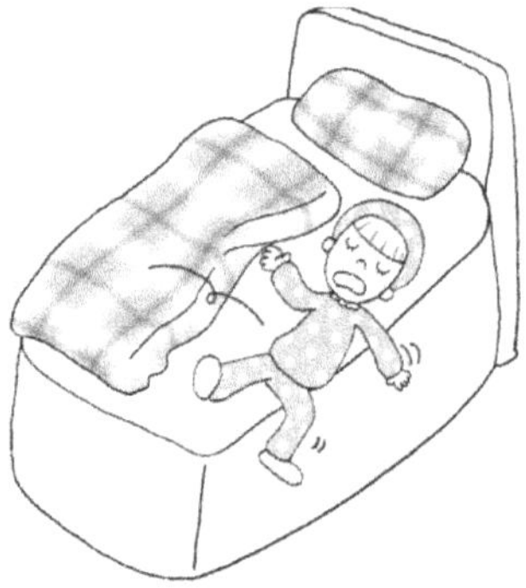

She sees the hedge and the ledge and has a big piece of leek on her teeth.

Sh-	Sheet	leek	Geek
An	And	Hand	Band
Sand	Wand	Rand	Land
You	Your	You are	You’re
Hop	Mop	Cop	Mob
Cob	Lob	Sob	Nob
Cod	Sod	Sop	Lot
Bob	God	Dog	Log

There is a rubber band in your hand.

There is a wand in your hand.

You have rand in your hand as you hop on the land.

You’re hip. You can hop. You’ve got a mop in your hand.

Bob	God	Dog	Log
Cop	Sop	Lop	Pop
Mop	Mob	Sob	Hop

The cops are in the bag.

The cobs are in the bag.

The mops are not in the bag.

That is good.

Has	Have	Eat	Heat
Meat	Seat	Weave	Beat
An	-ank	Bank	Thank
For	Fore	More	Core

He has yen. She has yen.
They have a yen for yen.
They have wads of yen.
They beat the bank.
They weave hats in the heat.
They thank you for the yen.

Hope	Hop	Lope	Lop
Pope	Pop	Cope	Cop
Away	Say	Lay	Bay
Many	Zany	Lady	Hazy
Hi	Pi	Di	Lady Di

The funny lady gives hope to many people.

He hopped on the car full of hope.

My pop taught me how to cope.

Bob loped away from the cops.

Any	Amy	Zany	Many
Hi	Pi	Di	Lady

The zany lady said hi to the cop.
Then she said, “Hi Di, what’s pi?”

Sell	Hell	Well	Bell
Heat	Meat	Seat	Feat
Mean	Meal	Heal	Seal

The hats sell well in the heat.
They have a bell on a seat.
They eat meat. What a feat.

-ai	Bait	Maid	Said
Laid	Raid	Wait	Paid
Want	Wall	Was	Walk
Say	Hay	Lay	May
Pond	Fond	Bond	Nod
Get	Bet	Set	Let

Mugmug has a bait. She wants fish.
She wants to eat fish in May.
She puts the bait in the pond and waits.
She may get a fish; she may not.

All	Tall	Call	Mall
Small	Smell	Smelter	Smash
Smart	Smoke	Smolder	Smug
Heart	Learn	Yearn	Ball
Time	Dime	Lime	Chime
Could	Know	Knew	Help
Burn	Turn	Churn	Church

The lady was small but she had a big heart. She yearned to learn but had no time, and so envy smoldered in her heart until she could hold it no longer. She was smart but when she smashed the baseball bat onto the table she knew it was time for her to seek help.

Mat	Mate	Fat	Fate
-ing	Be	See	Win
Also	Late	Rate	Kate
Wait	Bait	Gait	Maid

Being a fast runner is my fate.

Winning is also my fate.

Kate is my mate.

Over there she waits.

Cup	Mug	Jug	Rug
Beer	Deer	Cheer	Bug
Some	Come	Home	Rome
Can	Pan	Glad	Glass
Sit	Sitting	Stand	Standing

A can of cola, a cup of tea, and a jug of water are on the rug.

The deer cheers. The bug juggles some balls.

They feel at home in Rome – those two!

Keep	Weep	Seep	Beep
Law	Paw	Saw	Raw
Of	Off	Doff	Coffs
Side	Wide	Ride	Chide
Has	Have	Had	Hand

Keep your paws off my raw fish.

The law is on my side.

You do not have to weep.

Keep your hands to your side, doff your hat, and get a ride home to Coffs.

Ate	Rate	State	Gate
Late	Sate	Hate	Tate
Pull	Full	Fill	Pill

The boy, Tate, ate late at the gate.

The state took him away; he is full of hate.

He took his pill; he ate his fill.

We pulled him away but he came back anyway.

Ail	Sail	Pail	Mail
Tail	Bail	Wail	Fail

The sail failed to open up.

We looked at the tail of the ship.

What ailed this boat?

We bailed out in a pail with our mail on our laps.

Ark	Dark	Bark	Park
Lark	Remark	Clark	Shark

The shark in the ark is sharp.

"The ark is in the park," says Clark.

He may have said it on a lark.

Let us not bark in the park. It is dark.

Own	Blown	Thrown	Known
Nothing	Every	Going	Naughty

I own nothing.

I am not naughty.

I have known everyone going down that lane.

All	Call	Small	Fall
Ball	Tall	Pall	Mall
Save	Rave	Wave	Shave
Could	Would	Should	Couldn't
Ice	Rice	Price	Dice

All the calls, all the balls, could not save us.
We shaved and waved and raved at the cave.
We should not have gone to Pall Mall.
We would have saved some balls.
It's a small price to pay.

Bone	Clone	Scone	Shone
Tone	Lone	Phone	Gone

The clone of the bone shone inside the scone.
The tone of the lone cowboy was shrill on the phone.

Act	Tact	Pact	Aft
Fact	Draft	Craft	Taft
Say	Stay	Pay	Play

The fact is that if you act with tact you can get a pact. You do not have to be crafty, or play in the aft. You have to stay in the open and pay the price.

Road	Toad	Goad	Load
Day	Say	Ray	May
Light	Sight	Might	Right
-ing	Thing	Sing	Ring

Do not goad the toad on the road.
Do the right thing.
Sing with all your might.
Let the singing ring out and keep your eyes on the prize, not the price.

Pass	Lass	Glass	Grass

The lass has a glass in her hand.

The grass is green.

Bit	Bite	Sit	Site
Shin	Shine	Tim	Time
Down	Clown	Frown	Brown

Tim bit the shin of the guy who tried to run him down. What a clown! Down he went! Tim had won this time.

Feed	Feet	Feel	Peel
Street	Sweet	Tweet	Twig
Myself	Yourself	Himself	Herself

You are on Sweet Street.

You can feed yourself.

You peel wads of cash from your pockets.

You are yourself.

You do not feel like a twig.

You can tweet like a bird.

You're on Sweet Street.

Ought	Bought	Sought	Fought
Guy	Buy	What	Who

You sought, fought and bought what you wanted. What a guy! Who is it for? Won't you tell?

Batch	Catch	Thatch	Watch
Roof	Hoof	Wood	Good
Rob	Robber	Robbers	robbing
Try	Pry	Cry	Wry
The	They	Their	There

We catch a batch of robbers every day. We watch a bunch of robbers on our roof every night. We see them take good wood away every time. We try to catch them on the hoof. We pry into their lives and they cry like little babes.

Rest	Best	Test	Crest
Forest	West	Chest	Lest
Ward	Forward	Onward	Backward
Pound	Round	Sound	Mound

We rest in the forest lest we forget our crest. Onward ever, backward never; that is our cry. We are the best; where are the rest? Where is our test? We pound our chests.

Nine	Line	Pine	Dine
Chime	Crime	Prime	Drive
Fight	Light	Sight	Right

We dine in a line on the pines at nine.
In our prime, we fight; we drive.
We don't just fight; we do fight crime.
We've seen the light; our sight is clear.
As we do right, the church bell chimes.

Like	Likely	Time	Timely
Present	Absent	Yesterday	Today

It is likely that you will like the timely present from your friend. She sent it yesterday. I got it today. What will you send her in return?

Rush	Brush	Crush	Hour
Rush hour	Food	Tooth	Toothbrush
Would	Could	Should	Lost

In the crush of rush hour traffic, you lost your toothbrush. That was not so bad. How would it be if you had lost your tooth?

Dive	Hive	Jive	Wife
Knife	Knives	Wives	Five
But	Cut	Hut	Rut

He dives and jives and has five lives. He is alive, but in a hive. He has a hut; he's in a rut.

Eat	Feat	Meat	Seat
Team	Bream	Ream	Cream
Duck	Puck	Luck	Tuck

He eats his meat; he takes his seat.
He hits a puck; he eats his bream.
He eats his cream; he hits his puck.
He is in luck; he has a team.

Same	Name	Fame	Shame
Tame	Came	Wane	Sane
Left	Heft	Weft	Kept

The sharp looking singer I talked about?
She came in fame but left in shame.
She lost her charm; her fame did wane.

Yelp	Help	Kelp	Self
Carry	Carried	Himself	Herself

Mike yelped for help and got some kelp.
He carried it home all by himself.
His wife ate it all by herself.

Main	Gain	Lain	Rain
Week	Pain	Chain	Weak
Sure	Pure	Lure	Cure

He had lain there all week.

He was oh so weak.

He was sure in pain.

He could lure no one.

He could cure no one.

He was pure but in chains.

The rain beat down on him.

Hazy	Lazy	Crazy	Lady
Cot	Cod	Time	Gone

On a hazy day, the crazy, lazy lady lies in her cot, eats cod, and dreams of fun times gone by.

Might	Blight	Sight	Bright
Plight	Fright	Light	Fight
Joy	Enjoy	Hand	Chance

If you want to fight, you need the might.
Don't be frightened; set your sights high.
Don't let fright rob you of your chance to enjoy the bright lights.

Boot	Boom	Book	Boost
There	Then	This	That
These	Those	Boom box	Booth
Much	Such	Rush	Mush

You read a book; you got the boot.
You had your boom box in your booth.
Then the boss gave you the boot.
"Looks like you were having too much fun!"

Pile	File	Rile	Tile
Mile	Wile	Bile	Line
High	Sigh	Nigh	Wonder
Rise	Wise	Kite	Bite

There are piles of tiles one mile high.

You sigh and wonder what a pile.

You hold the line but you are riled.

You bite your lip and feel the bile.

You are wise, you think, you keep your cool.

Time	Dime	Mime	Chime
Lime	Shine	Mine	Pipe

For a dime or a lime you make it shine.

You are a mime in the pipe of a mine.

You get the bells to chime aright.

You get the bells to chime and shine.

Teen	Keen	Seen	Preen
Tween	Between	Colleen	Been
Either	Neither	Ever	Never

Colleen is neither here nor there.

Is she a teen? Is she a kid?

She preens all day, keen to be seen.

Is she a tween? Is she a teen?

Ride	Pro-	Provide	Profile
Bromide	Combine	Alive	Survive
Side	Reside	Coincide	Aside

Who provided the bromide?

What is your profile?

When do we get a ride?

Which of the cats is alive?

Are you sure we will survive?

You better pray and play and pray.

Take	Sake	Lake	Make
Cake	Bake	Made	Wade
Low	Shallow	Hallow	Callow
Ground	Found	Sound	Bound
Today	Tomorrow	Yesterday	Next

For my sake and yours.

Take the cake that you made.

Let us not wade into the shallow lake.

This is hallowed ground.

We are bound to bake a better cake someday.

Do not weep.

Tomorrow will be a better day.

Smart	Smack	Smooth	Small

She is small but very smooth.

She smacked me; I was too smart.

Goal	Foal	Shoal	Coal
Pick	Sick	Lick	Nick

The goal of the foal on the shoal is to pick up and lick the coal.

Need	Weed	Seed	Feed
sheep	Keep	Beep	Seep

We need the seeds in the weed to feed the sheep.

Too	Oops	Coop	Loop
Hoof	Hoot	Toot	Soot
Foot	Boot	Root	Moot
Suzuki	Honda	Fukuda	Fukui
Take	Lake	Shake	Fake

You too can get in the loop by tooting your own horn. Shake the soot off your boots. Fake it till you make it, so they say.

Mini-	Maxi-	Mum	Tub
Rub	Cub	Cut	Rut
Wage	Rate	Cage	Sage

What is the minimum wage?

What is the maximum rate?

Who is your favorite sage?

Why are you in a cage?

Get out of your rut.

Cut the cord or get out of the way.

Thin	Thing	Think	Thrill
Thirst	Thrust	Thought	Thank

The thin egghead was thrilled to be working at the think tank. She thrust the quill into my hands and thanked me for quenching her thirst.

Ace	Place	Race	Trace
Brace	Face	Lace	Cave
Bill	Hill	Chill	Fill
Mill	Till	Will	Sill
Calm	*Palm	Alms	Palms

*l in "Palm" may or may not be silent

He is an ace in the race. He has braces on, and a cave for a face. Still, the calm on his face says he will win. Chill out.

Age	Page	Sage	Wage
Know	Knee	Kneel	Knit
Brow	Brown	Crown	Knelt

Do you know the age of the sage?
He put his wages on his knee and knit his brows.

You	Cod	Gum	Gap
-ai	Bait	Maid	Said
Laid	Raid	Wait	Paid
All	Hall	Call	Mall
Want	Wall	Was	Walk
Say	Hay	Lay	May
Day	Way	Ray	Nay
Lazy	Hazy	Woozy	Baby

Wenwen said, "I do not want to be a maid!"
Mom said, "You mean you do not want to be a cook."

Wenwen said, "If you say so, mom."

Jay is on the hay all day.
He is lazy.
He looks woozy. Look at him.

-ai	Bait	Maid	Said
Way	Away	To	Day
Today	Say	Bay	Sashay
-ed	Seated	Heated	Fro
From	Froth	Frost	Frugal
Front	Friend	Free	Fresh

We are seated on a heated bed.
We are frugal; so we say.

We sashay towards the bay.
To and fro, to and fro.
Every day and every night.
Towards the bay.
We make our way.

-oa	boat	moat	load
Road	Roach	Roam	Loam
Ch-	Chiba	chop	chip
-ill	chill	-imp	chimp
Saw	Law	Raw	Thaw
Cell	Call	Hell	ill

On the road to Chiba I saw a chimp.
It lay on the road.
Feeling the chill.

On the road to Chiba, hopping along the loam, the chimp saw me, and licked its lips. Where are the cops? Where is the law?

Who	What	Where	Which
Why	How	Now	Bow
Pop	Mop	Top	Cop
Ill	Fill	Till	Sill

Where are the cops?
The chimp looked ill.
I took my cell and made a call.
The chimp jumped into my car and drove away.

Jump	Lump	Bump	Chump
Coat	Throat	Boat	Moat
Water	Wall	Round	Around

What a chump to jump around with a lump in his throat. The boat was on the moat; the coat was in the water.

all	Wall	Was	Walk
Say	Hay	Lay	May
Clap	Clam	Class	Club
Clue	Clot	Cling	Cleats

Clap your hands.

A clam is in the class!

Why, I have no clue.

Cling to your cleats, anyway.

Join the club now, not in May!

Sag	Wag	Lag	Nag
She	Sheep	Shop	Shot
Short	Shock	Shoot	Shin

The bag sags.

He lags.

We are sad that he is a nag.

All	Sad	Mad	Fun
Ate	Bun	Gun	Sun

He is sad.

We are all sad.

She is fun.

I am mad that she ate my bun.

Shy	Sty	Shop	Ship
Shinkawa	Shinagawa	Shinjuku	She
Good	Hood	Stood	Mood

The pig in the sty is mad.

No, it is shy.

It is fun.

It is going into a shop in Shinkawa, but I am on

my way to Shinjuku.

What mood are you in?

I am in the mood for good food in Shinjuku.

Men	Pen	Den	Hen
And	Stand	Strand	Strap
Very	Cherry	Merry	Terry
Full	Bull	Pull	Ink

The hen is in a pen.

The men are in a den.

A man stood on a beam and took a strap to the hen.

It was bad. The hen took a pen.

A pen full of ink is what the merry hen took.

She drew a cherry on a sheet.

Has	Was	Too	Fun
Drop	Drip	Drum	Drubbing
Dracula	Drama	Dramatic	Drastic

He was fun.

She was fun.

Ai-chan was fun.

The pig was fun.

The hen was fun too.

We won a hen.

It was a big hen.

A pig and a hen?

No, only a hen.

-ing	Wing	Ring	King
Swing	Swig	Swill	Swim
Wine	Wipe	Well	Bell
Swine	Swipe	Swell	Swollen
Morn	Morning	Eve	Evening
Night	Right	Sight	Light
Hare	Stare	Bare	Care

I like to swing in the morning.
I like to swim in the evening.
I feed my swine at night.
Swill some cola too.
This swine of mine just stares and stares.
As if I were the swine, you see.
That's when I say, "My dear swine, do you want to take a swig?"

Drop	Drip	Drum	Drubbing
Dracula	Drama	Dramatic	Drastic
After	For	Before	With

I need a drop of oil.

I want drips of oil in my drum.

A full drum is what I want.

That is drastic, isn't it? Not at all.

Far	Fare	Car	Care
Bar	Bare	Mar	Mare
Dart	Dare	Mart	Ware

We are far from home.

We do not care.

We have a mare.

It can dart.

I can dart into a mart and bring some wares.

Hour	Honor	Honey	Never
Clever	Sacrifice	Artless	Clueless
Freedom	Boredom	Seldom	Kingdom

In this hour of need, may we never forget to honor those who have sacrificed with honor to preserve our freedom.

Let	Bet	Set	Get
Drama	Coma	Sum	Summer
Queen	Quit	Quiz	Quinn

"Let us play drums after meals."

"Don't be such a drama queen."

"Why not, am I not a queen?"

"Cut it out. Cut it out."

"It's summer and it's hot. Can you stand the heat?"

"You bet."

Plan	Pluck	Plumb	Pleat
Please	Plough	Plaque	Place

I have a plan to pluck my plough from the farm. I plan to sell it and use the money to please my little girl in pleats.

She has to see the dentist to remove some of the plaque from her teeth.

Is money important? Money truly has its place.

Lay	Say	Day	May
Yes	Les	Des-	Mes-
Bessy	Messy	Dressy	This

"It is May," he says.

On this May day, he lay on a mat on the hay.

"May I go?" "Yes, Les, you may go. You are too messy."

Can you write?

The boy and the gal are in the car.

This toy is cool.

That woman is shy.

These pigs are hot.

Those pants are big.

They want rain.

There is good law in Panama.

We eat meat all day long.

The queen will quit her job today.

I fell into a coma when I tried to write a comma.

All is well in the fall.

Not so much in the dead of winter.

I have a spring in my step in the spring.

Is there blue glue pasted across the blue, blue sky?

Days of the week

Sunday

Monday

Tuesday

Wednesday

Thursday

Friday

Saturday

Sunday

Can you read? Can you write?

Who are you?

What is funny?

Why are you not mad?

When will you kiss the moon?

Where is my banana?

Which bandana is yours?

While you wait, have a banana.

Span	Spam	Spoon	Spook
Spy	Spry	Sprite	Spiel
Prepare	Prepay	Promote	Provoke

The horse was spooked when the spy spanked it, not once, but twice. As the horse took off the spry old lady, the spy, jumped onto the animal's back and took out her soft drink. "I better start preparing my spiel," she said.

Get	Bet	Net	Set
Got	Bit	Not	Sit
Hit	Lit	Wit	Pit
Use	Fuse	Muse	Accuse

The man bit the dog.

The dog bit the cat.

The cat in the net?

Yes, the cat in the net.

Set the net.

Sit on it.

When you fall into the pit, use your wit.

You may chat with your muse. That's one way to buy some time.

You may be accused, so have fun while you can.

Wig	Big	Fig	Gig
Let	see	Net	Sing
Song	Long	Wong	Kong

Is it a big wig or a wiglet?

It is a wiglet. It is on a piglet in a singlet.

What a gig!

Let us go and see.

Umpire	Umbrella	Umpteen	Pump

The umpire took the pump for the umpteenth time.

See	Fee	Tee	Wee
Tot	Dot	Cot	Rot

Do you see the tot in the cot?

Yes, I see a wee tot in a cot with a dot.

No, it is not a dot. It is a rot in the cot.

1-2-3

One is not fun.

Two are fun for sure.

Three even more so? Perhaps.

Four can be a merry bunch.

Five can be funny, chummy, and fun.

Six cannot fit in a car.

Seven can go on a boat.

Eight can swim all day.

Nine can shop till the end of the day.

Months of the year

January

February

March

April

May

June

July

August

September

October

November

December

Can you read? Can you write?

January is for me.

February is for you.

March is for her.

April is for him.

May is for the gals.

June is for the boys.

July is for the women.

August is for the men.

September is for all animals.

October is for the plants.

November is for you and me.

December is for one and all.

Ail	-ing	Rail	Sail
Buy	Guy	This	That
Buys	They	Hen	Then
Hail	Wail	Nail	Tail

The ailing pig is on the rail.
The top dog is sailing on a ship.
There is a nail in the sail.
The cat wails in the hail.

-wer	-ver	-ger (singer/wager)	-er
-nal	-ner	-ter	-mer
-ber	-cer	-ler	-cer

Number
Tanner
Cancer
Meter
Bummer

Shaver
Hatter
Ladder
Mother
Father

-wer	-ver	-ger(singer/wager)	-er
-nal	-ner	-ter	-mer
-ber	-cer	-ler	-cher(teacher)

Letter	Wander
Setter	Wanderer
Better	Wonder
Matter	Loner
Wetter	Former
Seller	Farmer
Fencer	Teacher
Singer	Fixer
Brewer	Broker
Manager	Blogger

Cardinal numbers

1. One
2. Two
3. Three
4. Four
5. Five
6. Six
7. Seven
8. Eight
9. Nine
10. Ten
11. Eleven
12. Twelve
13. Thirteen
14. Fourteen
15. Fifteen
16. Sixteen
17. Seventeen
18. Eighteen
19. Nineteen
20. Twenty

Can you read? Can you write?

Day

Night

Everyday

Tomorrow

Last week

Last month

This year

Last year

Every week

Every month

Every year

Every other day

Two days ago

Several days ago

A few weeks ago

Bit	Bite
Sit	Site
Pip	Pipe

The lad bit me last night.

He bites me every day.

Pamela sits at the site all day.

Pip has a pipe in his hand.

Hid	Hide
Win	Wine
Dim	Dime

She hid in the dark; she likes to hide in the dark.

He wins at the club every year.

His eyes can see a dime in a dim saloon.

Din	Dine
Kit	Kite
Sin	Sine
Bid	Bide

Can we dine in the din?

He has a kit for a kite.

If you like math you know that sine is not a sin.

Slim	Slime
Slid	Slide
Tim	time
Know	Knee

Tim bides his time to make the bid.

He is a slim slime-ball.

I slid on the hill last time; today I do not want slip or slide.

Time and tide waits for no man (or woman).

Prim	Prime	*Psalm	*Cupboard
Tim	Time	*Raspberry	*Receipt

*silent p

She looks prim; she is in her prime.

Tim can tell the time.

Grim	Grime	*Debt	*Doubt
Fin	Fine	*Dumb	*Crumb
Pin	Pine	*Numb	*Thumb
Ace	Face	*Climb	*Bomb
Full	Filled	*Lamb	*Comb
Soup	*Coup	*Silent b	*Silent b
Mad	Made		

*silent p

The grim face of the Grinch was full of grime.

There is a fine fin in your soup.

This pin is made of pine.

No debts to pay?

I have my doubts.

Rid	Ride	*Kneel	*Knowledge
Rip	Ripe	*Knife	*Knight

*Silent k

He took my bike; he rid me of my ride.

So much for a knight on a robust steed!

She ripped up my ant farm; she is ripe for jail.

Here is the knife she used, you see?

Mine	*Sign	*Foreigner	*Reign
Wide	*Diaphragm	*Campaign	*Gnome
Rise	Wise	Such	Much

*Silent g

That book is mine.

Look at the sticker on the cover.

The road to Hope, Arkansas[1], is wide.

Who can rise at five? Such a one is wise.

Who can bathe a gnome?

Such a one, a fool.

[1] ˈär-kən-ˌsȯ; *1 or* är-ˈkan-zəs

Bat	Bate	Can	Cane
Sure	Pure	Lure	Every

John Bates likes to say he is a bat.

Can you cane a bad guy?
Sure you can. You can lure him with a pure-looking cane.

Man	Mane	*Mustn't	*Soften
Pat	Pate	*Listen	*Fasten
Nap	Nape	*Christmas	*Chestnut
Pan	Pane	*Watch	*Catch
Pal	Pale	*Whistle	*Castle
Some	Come	Cap	Cape
Map	Maps	*Silent t	*Silent t

A lion's mane, a bald man's pate.
A tiger's nape on a Christmas morn.

Pat	Pate	Crane	Lane
Nap	Nape	Wan	Wane
Pan	Pane	Ban	Bane
The	Their	Shoe	Shoot

The man has a mane.

Pat's pate is shiny.

I took a nap; I put some oil at the nape of my neck.

Do you like rap?

Jolie hit the pane with a pan.

My good pal looks pale today.

Some like their omelets hot.

Neck	Deck	Check	Wreck

I craned my neck to see the check on the deck in the wreck.

This	Their	You	Your
Myself	Yourself	Our	Ourselves
Themselves	Himself	Herself	While
Wing	Thing	Sing	Ring

I will do it myself.

You can do your thing yourself.

They can’t come by themselves.

We will need to do it ourselves.

She put on the ring by herself.

He put on the tie by himself.

Mar	Mare	Dam
Grass	Raze	Grass
Dam	Dame	Mar
Sally	Sale	Work
Down	Clown	*Handsome
*Handkerchief	*Wednesday	Dame
Raze	Mare	Worm

*Silent d

The mare marred the fun at the party.

It was a Wednesday.

"Raze down the hut; it is for clowns," she cried.

"Oh no! We need to boogie down," said the worm. This was no ordinary party.

Soon the dame of the house was on her way, waving her handkerchief. "Stop that mare, stop that mare!" she cried.

Madam soon made it home, brimming with excitement. "Let us get to work," she said.

Sing	-ing	Ring	Ringlet
Bell	Sell	Well	Fell
Ear	Eye	Nose	Mouth
Sore	Bore	Lore	Core

Ronaldo likes to sing in the rain.

There is a ringing in my ear.

My mouth is sore.

I know the lore of the land but I don't want to bore you.

Keep your eyes open; keep your ears open.

You will get to the core.

The pig is singing and ringing a bell.

He fell on the bell. Oops!

*Depot	*Debut	*Gourmet	*Ballet
*Chalet	*Buffet	*Valet	*Often

*Silent t

The valet is a gourmet cook.
He made his debut as a chef at the depot.
There was a ballet performance.
The buffet was oh so splendid.

Bell	Sell	Well	Fell
Ear	Eye	Nose	Mouth
Ring	Sing	Wing	Ding

We sell pigs and hens.

He is a singer.
She is a ringer.

Head	Dead	*Read	*Lead
Water	Butter	Oil	Foil
Use	Fuse	Muse	Abuse
Short	Port	Sort	Dork

*Also, Read (past tense)
*Also, Lead (metal)

There is dead hair on my head.

I read a story yesterday, which said that there was lead in the foil that we use every day.

Water	Butter	Oil	Foil
Use	Fuse	Muse	Abuse

Do not abuse the lass; she has a short fuse.

He is a dork but a muse of sorts.

But	Cut	Bug	Mug

The bug is on the mug, but he cannot see it.

This hen is in the cot of the tot.

The bug is not on the mug; it is on my leg.

Fear	Tear	Dear	Clear
Rear	Sear	Tears	Wear
Ride	Pride	Side	Slide

My dear, do not fear.

You are in the clear.

Do not tear yourself apart.

Do not go to the rear.

You will be seared.

Do not shed any tears.

Wear your kimono now.

I am at your side.

Sing	Ring	Wing	Ding

We sing in a ring.

A ding-dong song.

With wings and rings we sing and sing.

Story	Lorry	Sorry	Carry
Marry	Tarry	Barry	Larry
Cause	Be	Because	Before

Barry and Carrie have a story to tell.

They want to get married in Hawaii.

It takes a lot of planning.

They have talked to their family and friends.

Everyone wants to come along.

They may need two airplanes.

If they say yes to everyone.

Mend	Tend	Send	Lend
Wend	Bend	Rend	Blend
Thought	Bought	Fought	Sought

Ben tends to bend my ears every day.
Wending his way through a story or two.
Sending me into the land of sleep and dreams.
Rending my mind.
Blending my thoughts with his own.
I bought a pail for my mother.
Fought again with my sister.
Sought a present for my brother.
Thought again, and went to sleep.

Void	Avoid	Oil	Toil
Voice	Choice	Noise	Royce
Heard	Beard	Yearn	Earn

When I heard my Papa's voice.

I yearned to go for a drive.

Boss	Ross	Moss	Loss
Mind	Find	Bind	Lost
Money	Funny	Sunny	Runny
Rolling	Bone	Stone	Gather

My boss, Ross, lost his mind.

He had been funny and sunny before.

He is now in a sort of a bind.

Tittering and tattering and walking pitter-patter all day long.

Goal	Goat	Boat	Foal

A baby goat is not a foal.

It is a kid.

Do you have a goal to buy a boat?

Not with no money in your coat pocket.

Home	Dome	Cone	Tone

From my home, which is, a dome.

Comes a tone. I mean, a tome.

From the cone, the attic bright, comes the ring of a mobile phone.

Bed	Ned	Let	Set
Wed	Wet	Ten	Get

Ned let the bed get wet again.

Ted set ten beds upon his back.

Hiss	Miss	Piss	Kiss
Snake	Bake	Cake	Take
Took	Book	Cook	Look

Tanaka took the cake to the snake.

The snake hissed and took a look.

Tanaka said, "I baked this cake."

The snake kissed him.

"Thanks, my bud."

In	Sing	Single	Mingle
Tingle	Dingle	Jingle	Crinkle

Makoto is single.

He likes to mingle.

He tickles the ivory, feels a tingle, makes a jingle and crinkles his brow.

He likes singing solo.

Panda	Santa	Wanda	Wander
Like	Bike	Ride	Gripe

The panda, Miranda, likes to wander.

The panda, Miranda, likes his ginger drink.

The panda, Miranda, rides his bike.

The panda, Miranda, has his gripes.

Belt	Felt	Welt	Pelt
Knelt	Pelted	Stone	Scones

Sandy knelt down to pray.

She felt good about the day.

She touched her belt.

She touched her skin.

She felt the welts grow on her arm.

She ate a scone.

"I need to pray more and more," she said.

More	Core	Sore	Bore
Less	Bess	Mess	Tess

Less is more.

And more is less.

Bess is sore, Tess a bore.

If more is less and less is more.

What's the core of the less that is more and the more that is less?

What's the score for Bess and Tess?

Rice	Price	Lice	Dice
Day	Say	May	Today

What's the price of rice today?

Why so many lice today?

Why the dice on the ice?

Numb	Thumb	Number	Lumber
Slumber	Plumber	Mamba	Samba

Samba Mamba is a plumber.

She likes to slumber on the lumber and listen to a samba number.

Her thumb is numb from all the plumbing.

Her slumber long, from all the samba numbers danced.

She is Samba Mamba and she is a plumber.

Food	Mood	Wood	Shoot
Poodle	Noodle	Doodle	Wheedle
Paris	Manila	Canary	London
Share	Shape	Ship	Shop

The poodle, *Paris*, is in London.

Eating noodles, making doodles.

When *Paris* is in a good mood, she shares her food with the canary, *Manila.*

Uncle	Undo	Unguent	Untie
Unorthodox	Unsaid	Unassuming	Uncouth

That uncle of yours has an unorthodox way of applying the unguent to his elbow. Some might say he is uncouth in the way he talks or that he leaves a lot unsaid.

Eat	Each	Teach	Reach
Preach	Teacher	Preacher	Breach
Poach	Coach	Poacher	Loafer

The teacher is a preacher and an eater.
He preaches and he teaches.
He is a poacher, but a teacher and a preacher all the same.

He coaches and he poaches; he is a preacher, a teacher, a poacher, and a loafer.

Few	Dew	Pew	Whew
People	Freeze	Freezing	Wheezing

There is dew on the pews.

Few people are in the pews.

People are freezing in the pews.

There is wheezing and freezing.

There are few lads and lasses in the pews.

Ever	Never	Clever	River
Better	Bitter	Litter	Letter
Liver	Shiver	Eaten	Beaver
Watch	Catch	Watches	Catches

Are you clever?

Have you ever eaten liver?

Do you litter?

Are you bitter?

Can you write a better letter?

Ever	Never	Clever	River
Better	Bitter	Litter	Letter
Liver	Shiver	Eaten	Beaver
Watch	Catch	Watches	Catches

Can you swim in a river?

Or do you shiver in the river?

While the river beaver watches you?

Can	Cancer	Dancer	Lancer
Who	What	Which	When

This lancer is a dancer who likes to banter.

He is not the only lancer, nor the only dancer who has fondness for minced meat.

Which of the dancers or the lancers do you want to see today?

Low	Blow	Slow	Flow

Go with the flow.

Make it slow.

Do lie low.

Rag	Drag	Dragon	Dragging

The dragon is dragging the rag away.

Ink	Rink	Drink	Shrink

The shrink is drinking ink on the rink.

Only	Boldly	Silly	Glumly
Billy	Chilly	Rally	Sally

Billy bought Sally a bag at the silly chilly rally.

Boldly and glumly he set off, the only one on that lonely road.

Is	Risk	Disk	Wisp
Brisk	Frisk	Crisp	Prism
Light	Sight	Fight	Fighter

Be brisk when you see that wisp of a boy.

He is light on his feet, a fighter true.

Don't take the risk of taking away his disk.

He can see you through his prism.

He will frisk you and beat you to a crisp.

Beam	Team	Ream	Seam
Empty	Void	Avoid	Humpty

This is the "A" Team.

They have reams of paper.

They have no seams at all.

They can beam you up into the empty void.

Cover	Lover	Mover	Rover
Plover	Stove	Stover	Goner

I have a cover.

I'm a lover, a mover and a rover.

I'm not a plover in a Rover.

Or a stover on a stove.

Cake	Lake	Take	Rake

Rake the cake from the lake, will you?

Dead	Head	Bread	Thread
Threat	Wish	Fish	Dish

He is a deadhead with a thread in his bread. He is no threat. His wish is to eat a dish of fish. Let him be, will you?

Old	Older	Colder	Folder
Once	Twice	Thrice	Mice
Beat	Meat	Feat	Seat

He is older. He feels colder.

From his velvet seat on high, with his folder on his lap, he can beat all the cunning mice.

Once, twice, or three times even.

What a feat for an old chap!

Cole	Sole	Role	Mole
Dole	Pole	Hole	Put

Old Cole's sole role is to put the mole in a hole.

Chaos	Chord	Cholesterol	echo

We do not like chaos.

Cholesterol can bring chaos into one's life.

Brag	Bran	Brand	Branch
Drag	Drank	Drab	Drip
Name	Same	Fame	Wane

I brag about my brand name goods.

But there are more important things in life.

I drag my bag.

I eat my bran.

I drink in drips at a branch of the bank, and eat my bran -- a brand-name bran.

An	Dan	Chan	Jam
Are	Who	Which	Why
Real	Really	Mere	Merely

Dan and Chan are in a jam.

Why? I don’t really know

Vary	Tarry	Starry	Carry
Night	Light	Fight	Right

We vary in how much we can carry.

We tarry on a starry night.

Fume	Fuse	Refuse	Refute

We fume and we fuse.

We refuse and refute.

Deny	Rely	Night	Sight

We rely on our sight.

We can fight in the night.

To uphold our rights.

*Honor	*Ghetto	*Ghost	*Heir

*Silent h

The ghost from the ghetto made sure that the heir had some honor.

Florida	Flat	Flee	Fluid
Pant	Flip	Lush	Mango
Flux	Flamingo	Flippant	Flush

Fumito fled on the flat Florida land.
He ran like a river true; I am not being flippant! He ate his mango and said hi to a flamingo, while running like there was no tomorrow.

Paper	Caper	Baker	Shaker
About	Around	House	Sound
Went	Vent	Sent	Dent

In the paper was a caper about a baker who went around the house denting the walls; he had a shaker in his hand that made funny sounds.

She	Eat	Meat	Neat
Ear	Hear	Wear	Rear
Shake	Bake	Rake	Take

I eat meat. She eats meat.

We hear neat singing in the rear.

My ear is ringing.

We wear earrings and we like to bake, rake and brake our lorries at the brink.

*Salmon	*Lincoln	*Colonel	*Folks
*Could	*Would	*Should	*Calf
*Salve	*Balm	*Calm	*Psalm
*Almond	*Half	Pound	*Walk
*Talk	*Walking	Bound	Around

*Silent l

Did Lincoln like to eat salmon? What a balm that would have been, walking and talking and eating almonds and half talking to himself.

Grow	Grill	Grass	Grin
Graze	Grate	Grab	Ground
Even	Ever	Every	Everyday

The kids grow fast.

The grass grows faster.

We grin when the cows graze on our grass.

We grab one for the summer; we grab one for the fall. We sure have a happy grill.

*Column	*Solemn	*Hymn	*Damn
*Autumn	Process	Procession	Concession
Whole	White	While	Why

*Silent n

We walked in a column singing solemn hymns. The autumn procession ended up at the concession. The whole process was a success. Why? I don't know.

Spat	Spit	Sport	Spell
Speak	Spill	Speech	Sprinkle
Try	Tried	Pry	Pried
Come	Came	Go	Went
Wrong	Wry	Wring	Wrought
Write	Writing	Writhe	Writhing

He fell while he was speaking, but he was a good sport.

He tried to spell "spill" but it came out all wrong. He sprinkled some water on the grass, played the fool as usual, and all was forgotten.

*Mnemonic	Memory	Memorial	Memoir

*Silent m

Mnemonics can help you remember when you want to write your memoirs.

Glut	Glib	Gleam	Glutton
Listen	Glisten	Glow	Globe
Night	Right	Tight	Sight
Quiet	Quite	Quick	Quibble

The globe glistens at night.

I see the gleam in your eyes when you see the pork glistening on the grill.

It is quite a sight to see you leap for the pork.

I do all I can to keep quiet. I do not want to quibble with you over meat; I am fond of meat myself. Next time, do not be so quick, okay?

*Illinois	*Island	*Aisle	*Debris
*Arkansas	Whether	Weather	Wet

*Silent s

Whether you are in Arkansas or Illinois[2].

Sometimes the weather gets a little wet.

You dream of taking off to an island where the aisles of the supermarkets are overflowing with juice.

Pack	Pick	Sick	Lick
Dick	Hick	Nick	Kick
Wick	Wacky	Jack	Jacky
People	Some	Others	Another
Because	Unless	Since	But

Some say Jack is a hick because he has a wick in his ear.

Others say he is wacky because he licks pickles every day.

Don't kick Jack around, people; he may be sick but he sure packs a punch.

[2] i-lə-ˈnȯi *or* -ˈnȯiz

House	Mouse	Rouse	Douse
Louse	Around	Abound	Amount
Moves	Goes	Does	Loves

There is a mouse in the house.

It moves around all day.

It goes round and round. It loves to rouse me from my sleep. I am at my wit's end. Joy!

Brow	Browse	Brown	Browbeat
Raise	Maize	Wait	Hail
Phone	Photo	Philosophy	Philip
Harass	Photograph	All	Ball

Sheila browsed around the bookstore. She raised an eyebrow when she saw a man with maize on his head. The man tried to browbeat her but he was no match for Sheila, who called the cops on her cell phone. It was Sheila's philosophy to photograph anyone who tried to harass her.

Free	Freedom	Seldom	Bore
Boredom	London	Tom	Atom
Like	Hike	Dike	Mike

Tom likes to be free.

He likes his freedom.

He is seldom bored.

He likes to hike.

He gets on the dike.

Like an atom, he flits around.

Day	Say	Lay	Way
Cay	May	Nay	Bay

“Mayday, mayday,” they say.

It’s the way of the cay and the bay in May.

Lick	Pick	Slick	Tick
Mick	Sick	Wick	Kick
Cream	Clean	Ice	Rice
Each	Reach	Peach	Teach

Mick is slick.

He picks and ticks his candle wicks each day.

He seldom kicks the sick.

He likes to lick his ice cream clean.

Photo	Orphan	Philip	Philosophy
Elephant	Him	Her	Himself

Philip is an orphan whose philosophy is to take a photo of himself every day.

Ought	Bought	Sought	Fought
Aid	Paid	Raid	Said

You ought to do the best you can.

You bought into some good ideas.

You sought to do the best you could.

You've fought the good fight -- good for you.

You said you'd aid others if you could.

You said you would not raid the fridge.

You do get paid when you do good work.

Asp	Rasp	Grasp	*Raspberry
Snake	Fake	Take	Wake

*Silent p

An asp is a snake.

Don't grasp the tail of the snake.

You will wake the snake and get a bite.

The cobra has eaten a raspberry.

Its voice is a bit raspy.

Health	Wealth	Stealth	Dealt

Health is wealth.

Some people gain their wealth by stealth.

Lick	Flick	Rick	Prick
Blood	Flood	Finger	Singer

Rick licked the yogurt on his index finger.

He watched some flicks; he sang some songs.

Few	Knew	Drew	Blew
Threw	Hew	Dew	Lewd
Bristle	Brim	Brave	Bravo
Head	Heady	Heavy	Wood

Few knew that Drew blew away the bucks, and threw away the wood that he had hewn.

Weak	Leak	Beak	Peak
Bleak	Pleat	Creak	Peat

Jackie is not weak.

He walked all the way to the peak,

which was covered with peat.

It was bleak looking at the beaks of the birds and watching the creaking, leaking roofs.

Brew	Brilliant	Bread	Break
Bristle	Brim	Brave	Bravo

Tanaka makes a brilliant brew.

It's a sort of milk for babes.

He fills a bottle to the brim and hands it over to the baby, who bristles at first but soon says, "Yum, yum, yum!"

Are	Art	Arm	Article

We are who we are.

We love art; we hate arms.

All	Tall	Call	Mall
Walk	Walked	Jump	Jumped
Tough	Rough	Cough	Might
Fight	Right	Sight	Light
Round	Around	Lout	Bout

Two tall men walked and jumped around in the mall. They tried not to fall but it was slick in there. It was tough and rough but they kept their eyes on the prize, the "Stay on Your Feet" award. When it was done, they said, "Do not lose sight of your goal. Keep your eyes on the light at the end of the tunnel."

Ear	Hear	Tear	Fear
Down	Clown	Well	Will

With your ears you can hear, but do not fear what you hear and tear yourself down for no good reason. All will be well if you do not fall.

Chip	Ship	Sharp	Short
Chiba	Chick	Chicken	Chill
Want	Some	Come	Because

She is in Chiba.

She has a chill in Chiba.

She is there because she wants to have a chicken meal.

Her	There	Were	Here
She	He	His	Him

She is in Aoyama. She is in Edogawa.

She is in Okinawa. She is in Shinjuku.

She is in Shibuya. He is in Akita.

He is in Nagoya. He is in Odaiba.

Can you read?

Who is Peter Pan?

What is your name?

Why are you so happy?

Which color do you like?

While you are in class do you daydream?

When is your birthday?

Where do you like to relax?

How are you today?

The sun is in the sky. This is what I like. These days I spend a lot of time in the sun. It may not be good for me but those doctors who advise me to stay out of the sun like to relax in the sun themselves. If they stop going to the beach on sunny days then I will stop sunbathing too. Otherwise, I will keep on loving the sun and living like the son of the sun. Bad, bad me.

Form	Dorm	Horn	Corn
One	Two	Three	Four
Dress	Press	Mess	Chess

He is in form one.

She is in form two.

She is in the dorm.

He eats corn.

Lay	Play	Say	Ray
Long	Song	Bong	Chong

She plays the horn.

She has her say all day long.

There she is with Doctor Chong.

Goes	Does	Any	More

There she goes.

She does not play the horn anymore.

Fore	Sore	Core	Pore

I am sore.

You are sore at the core.

My pores are sore.

This is going to be fun.

We are going to play all day.

Say no more.

Go to the fore.

All	Mall	Fall	Call

All of us are going to play.

Do not call me.

If you fall, go to the mall.

There's a nifty clinic somewhere there.

Doc	-tor	There	They
The	This	That	These
Those	Then	Thy	Thine

There is a doctor in the mall.

Call the doctors in the mall if you fall.

All the rectors will be there; the proctors will be there too.

But why?

Inquiring minds would love to know.

His	Her	He	Him
Rol	Col	Mal	Pal
Role	Cole	Male	Pale

My pal, Cole, is pale. What is his role? His role is to fall down the stairs.

Remember, this is a movie. Next time, he hopes to get a speaking role.

Ill	Will	Kill	Till
Just	Must	Bust	Lust
Pre-	-tend	-ing	Be

He is ill.

Is he? Not at all, you see.

He is just pretending to be sick.

-ool	Cool	Wool	Tool
Pool	Stool	Fool	Drool

He looks cool in wool and he has his tools all set.

He is not ill at all.

He is sitting on a stool and does not look anything like a fool.

Stop drooling; he is just eating a sandwich.

Has	Have	Ham	Hat

He has ham.

She has a hat on.

Hand it to me.

The hat? The ham?

We all have ham to eat.

But	Cut	Hut	Put
Crap	Crab	Cram	Crag
Crib	Cream	Crinkle	Crew

Cut the ham. Put it on the crab and eat it.

Get into the hut.

It is cool in there.

He put the cut of ham in a hat and ate it, all at once.

Ordinal numbers

1st	First	2nd	Second
3rd	Third	4th	Fourth
5th	Fifth	6th	Sixth
7th	Seventh	8th	Eighth
9th	Ninth	10th	Tenth
11th	Eleventh	12th	Twelfth
13th	Thirteenth	14th	Fourteenth
15th	Fifteenth	16th	Sixteenth
17th	Seventeenth	18th	Eighteenth
19th	Nineteenth	20th	Twentieth

Lack	Lock	Luck	Lick

I lack a lock but I am in luck.

You lick the lock and all is cool.

Tin	Pin	Win	Chin

Put a tin on your chin and we will win.

A tin or a pin?

No way I will put a tin or a pin on my chin!

-ick	Sick	Rick	Lick
Pick	Nick	Chick	Wick
Name	Named	Same	Tame
Friend	Blend	Send	Tend

Rick is sick. He puts on the same clothes all week long. He has a friend named Wick in his house. This Wick, this pet, I mean, is tame. It cries cock-a-doodle-doo.

How does it look?

Beautiful	Pretty	Sharp	Ugly
Unbecoming	Attractive	Awkward	Gross
Lovely	Despicable	Appealing	Cute
Charming	Pleasing	Enthralling	Cool

What a lovely chap!
It is unbecoming of you to treat people badly.
Some might even say it's despicable to be mean.
What do you think?

Bum	Rum	Chum	Mum
Glad	Glum	Glib	Gloom

What a bum, but he is my chum.

I am glum when he is gloomy.

He is glib.

That makes me glad.

Cli-	Sli-	Sla-	Low
Click	Slick	Slack	Slow
Eel	-eel	Heel	Feel
Sleep	Fee	Feet	Sheep
Slay	Slew	Slim	Slit

He clicks his heel in the slick. He is slack and slow.

He is slower than a sheep in a shopping mall.

Ja-	Pan	Kyo-	To
Sen-	Ten	Pen	Men
Peg	Leg	Lens	Pencil

Japan Tokyo Kyoto

Tokyo is in Japan.

Kyoto is in Japan.

Nagoya is in Japan.

Sendai is in Japan.

She has a pen pal in Sendai.

I have a pen pal in Nagoya.

Or	For	Good	Wood
Food	Mood	Book	Room
When	Where	Why	What
Boon	Soon	Boom	Doom
Noon	Loon	Cool	Pool
Near	Fear	Rear	Hear
Worry	Sorry	Lorry	Merry

His mood is good when he has some food.

Where is my book? Is it in the room? Yes, it is.

Did you hear the boom?

What boom?

The boom at noon sounded like doomsday.

If you did not hear it, do not worry.

Be merry.

Buy	Guy	Eel	Feel
Ask	Task	Mask	Bask

The guy feels he has to buy eel.

Eating eel is good for you.

Bought	Fought	Sought	Wrought
Sweater	Change	Range	Strange

We bought a sweater and fought over the change. It was pretty strange for others to see two dwarves fighting over coins.

Ask	Task	Mask	Bask
What	Why	Who	Where
Whisk	Risk	Flask	Brisk

Ask him where the eel is.

It is in the room.

Why do you have a mask on? Why do you ask me why I have a mask on?

You	Your	Who	Where

Where is your mask?

Who is asking? I am.

Snake	Snack	Snail	Snooker
Play	Tray	Glade	Glide
Out	Bout	Gout	Rout

A snake and a snail played snooker one day. The snake had the snail for a snack. Ouch!

Cuddle	Muddle	Puddle	Huddle
Little	Pickle	Sickle	Colors

We cuddled in a huddle in the puddle after the muddle.

*Answer	*Wrap	*Sword	*Wrist
*Wrestle	*Write	*Wrote	*Written
Quest	Question	Queue	Quit

*Silent w

The wrestler has written the answer to the question on his wrist. He is planning to quit the quest for the title if he cannot get in the queue.

Get	Getups	Getaway	Gets
Gender	General	Gem	Geology
Winner	Sinner	Bidder	Winter

A geologist in her new getups gets to keep the gem she found while doing a general investigation. She says she is a winner because her gender has not been a barrier to her success.

Colors

Antique White	Gold	Royal Blue
Aquamarine	Gray	Salmon
Azure	Green	Scarlet
Bisque	Indigo	Seagreen
Black	Magenta	Sienna
Blue	Moccasin	Silver
Brown	Orange	Snow
Chartreuse	Peach	Spring Green
Chocolate	Peru	Tan
Coral	Pink	Teal
Cornsilk	Plum	Thistle
Crimson	Powder Blue	Tomato
Cyan	Purple	Turquoise
Dark Blue	Red	Violet
Fuchsia	Rosy Brown	White

-ock	Clock	Clack	Click
Tick	Tock	-ing	Cling
Click	Clack	Black	Slack
Blend	Bless	Bleed	Blimp

Click, clack, click.

Tick, tock, tick.

The clock ticks on.

But where is it?

On the book?

Not at all, in the black bag.

Who is clinging to the clock?

I feel it is an eel.

*Asthma	Patient	Office	Doctor

*Silent th

The asthma patient waited patiently for the doctor to arrive at the office.

Whose	One	Two	Three
Know	Knew	Knowledge	Kneel
Believe	Receive	Conceive	Down

Whose eel is it?

I wish I knew.

A singing eel?

I can't believe my ears.

Four	Five	Six	Seven
Wo-	Man	Men	Women

Four men in a cot.

Five eels in a pan.

Six books in a room.

Seven women on a log.

-ouse	Mouse	House	Rouse
From	Fry	Free	Frat

One mouse in a house.

Rouse the mouse from the frat house.

Do not fry the mouse. Be gentle, careful, and kind.

-ice	Ice	Mice	Lice
Are	Rice	Like	Hike

There is ice in the house.

There are mice in the house.

There are lice in the house.

There is rice to eat.

The mice like rice.

Yuko likes to hike.

Yuka is on the mike.

Yuki does not like lice.

Eight	Nine	Ten	Eleven
-en	Open	Door	Floor
Book	Look	Took	Nook

Eight pigs in a pen? Nine hens in a house?

Ten pins in a box? Eleven oxen in a hut?

Open the door.

Look at the floor.

He took the book from the floor for me.

List	Fist	Mist	Wrist
Make	Made	Lam	On
Saw	Face	Lace	Case

He made a fist.

There was a mist.

I saw his wrist.

I made a face behind the lace.

Cot	Got	Hot	Lot
Case	Face	Lace	Mace
Book	She	Shy	Shook

He got on my case.

He saw the list.

He shook his fist.

She bit his lip.

Make	Made	-ade	Lemon
Shall	Sham	Shark	Shabby
Business	Love	Keeps	Groceries

We made lemonade yesterday.

We are making lemonade today.

We shall make lemonade tomorrow.

Our business is not too shabby.

We love it.

It keeps us in groceries.

Sad	Mad	Had	Lad
Wad	Magazine	Lag	Gag
Ham	Sam	Dam	Map
Vat	Rat	Sat	Man

You may be mad and sad today.

You may not have wads of yen in your wallet today.

Don't cry. Tomorrow may be a better day.

Bib	Crib	Fib	Nib
Dig	Rig	Bin	Chin
Sit	Wit	Lit	Fit

The baby in the crib has a bib on.

The baby's grandma has a nib in her chin. She thinks it makes her charming.

-ing	Ink	Drink	Bring
Come	Came	Drank	Some
Lemon	-ade	Hand	Hang

Drink some lemonade.

The handsome lad drank some lemonade.

Come in.

Take my hand.

Hang in there.

Hand it to me.

She came; she saw; she conquered.

Thing	Think	Thin	Thimble
Prick	Primp	Prep	Pram

The thing about thimbles is that they are thin.

You have to think before you sew.

You could prick yourself badly without one.

You need that thingamajig – the thimble.

-wer	Flower	Cower	Power
Rower	Mower	Sower	Bower
Be	For	Fore	Before

Don't cower before the flower.

Don't be mean to the flower.

You may have the power.

You may mow the grass.

You may sow some seeds.

Whatever you do.

Think twice before you act.

Cry	Pry	Dry	Try
Cried	Pried	Dried	Tried
She	Shed	Wood	Food

I try to pry open the door of the dry woodshed.

I cry and cry till the cows come home.

Need	Feed	Seed	Weed

I need the food to feed my cat.

I pried and pried but had no luck.

-ad	Tad	Chad	Pad
Cad	Mad	Fad	Sad

Tad is in Chad.

He has a pad in Chad.

Tad is a sad lad and a cad.

He is mad at today's fad.

Is he a tad sad?

No, he is more than a tad sad.

Get	Let	Met	Set

Get me the pad.

Let me set it on the mat.

-ab	-rab	Crab	Drab
Crass	Crash	Cram	Grab

A drab crab on a test drive crashed his silver car.

I have to cram for the test after the crash course.

My friend is a crass cad who likes to eat crab.

Art	Bart	Cart	Dart
Fart	Mart	Tart	Artist

Bart throws darts.

He jumps on his cart and goes to the mart with his works of art.

He is an artist who likes to eat tarts.

Die	Died	Tie	Tied
Lie	Lied	Pie	Bow-tie
Lead	Leader	Plead	Pleader

The leader wears a tie.

The pleader wears a bowtie.

They eat their meat-pie.

They lie low sometimes.

They both plead for pies and ties.

High	Sigh	Nigh	Night
Winter	Hinterland	Winger	Splinter

In the winter he sighs at night.

Sitting on his high chair.

He lives in the hinterland.

He splinters wood.

He also plays hockey.

He calls himself a winger.

Had	Hid	Hug	Hum
Ray	Tray	Trick	Trip
Lay	Play	Pray	Pram
Baby	Babies	Carry	Carrying

What is a hod?

It is a tray.

What is a pram used for? It is used for carrying babies.

Ore	Pore	Sore	Core
Lore	Fore	Wore	Tore

What is the core of the lore?

I wish I knew.

Do you have ore in your pores?

Awn	Sawn	Pawn	Lawn

We were on the lawn when the wood was sawn into two.

We were looking at the awning when the pawnbroker came.

Tax	Lax	Fax	Pax
Max	Wax	Romana	Sax
Title	Collect	Collector	Floor

Pax Romana? What is that?

The tax collector is not lax.

Max plays the sax.

He waxed the floor and sent the fax.

Ray	Play	Say	Day

Ray plays tricks all day long.

Lay	Play	Pray	Pram

She lies in her pram and prays all day.

He hides the tray in the pram all night.

They play tricks on each other all month long.

Must	Rust	Bust	Dust
Rest	Test	Best	Lest

There is dust on the bust of the gladiator.

I must go. I want to meet the rest if I can’t see the best.

Gone	Done	Some	Come

We must not rest until the dust is gone from the bust.

Lest I forget, I need my rest.

End	Tend	Fend	Send
Attend	Scam	Scammer	Ram

Julie fends for herself.

She attends school every day.

She stays away from scammers.

She likes to draw a ram, a rose, and a spear at the end of each day.

Led	Ted	Sled	Fled
Bled	Pled	Wed	Red
Chase	Haste	Fast	Last
Thief	Thieves	Sieve	Wedding

Ted led the chase on the sled.

The robbers fled; they were in haste.

Ted carried a red flag and pled with the thieves.

“Bring back the sieves. They are for my wedding,” he said.

Drop	Prop	Crop	Mop
Dropped	Propped	Cropped	Mopped
Show	Shop	Ship	Ship

Wendy dropped the mop and took the prop, and then she cropped her hair for the show.

Cap	Ash	Cash	Lash
Flash	Flap	Lap	Lapland

He put some ash and some cash in his cap and pulled out a lash; he flashed the cap in his lap and said, “Let’s go to Lapland.”

Try	Pry	True	Trial
Trip	Trim	Triple	Trickle
Door	Open	Close	Liquid
Extra	Expect	Expected	Expo

When they tried to pry the door open a trickle of liquid began to flow.

When they went to trim their beards for the trip they were told to get ready for a truly close shave.

When they opened the door, they found triple the number of cards they expected for the expo.

Need	Seed	Feed	Weed
Indeed	Friend	Brand	Branch
Garden	Tough	Cough	Enough

We need some seeds to feed our friends.

The weeds in our garden are pretty tough.

You need to be tough to take them out.

If you stay too long you are sure to cough and that's enough to make you not come back for a long time.

Brad	Brat	Grad	Sad
Great	Treat	Party	Chart
Chap	Chat	Chip	Chop

Brad is a brat and a grad-to-be. Isn't that sad? No, it's great. What a treat to have him at our party. He is a great singer and he is on the charts.

Bum	Slum	Crum
Bumble	Crumb	Crumble
Drum	Beat	Teat
Love	Dove	Move

The bum lives in the slum.

He plays drums all day.

He eats crumbs.

He loves the drumbeat.

He has a dove or two.

Urge	Purge	Surge	Splurge
Ran	Rank	Ranks	Bank

We were urged to purge from our ranks those who splurged after the surge at the bank.

Call	Send	Make	Do
Recall	Resend	Remake	Redo
Company	Trouble	Strike	Strikes

"Recall, resend, remake, redo."

That's what companies do when trouble strikes.

Meat	Seat	Cheat

Jim is on a seat eating meat. He does not cheat.

Ant	Pant	And	Land
Want	Can't	Sand	Wand
Stand	Standard	Stamp	Start

Jim has ants in his waistband.

He can't stand it anymore.

He wants all the sand to play with.

That is standard with him.

He has his wand and his stamps and he wants to get at the ants at once.

He will land in hot water if he cannot beat the ants.

Stamping his feet and yelling do not help at all.

Past	Mast	Rest	Crest
Still	State	Stammer	Stuck
Vast	Last	Guest	First
Sticks	Stones	Steal	Stare

It's still not too late to stammer an apology to the state. Do not feel stuck because you said something stupid. Sticks and stones will break your bones but words of apology may mend a broken heart or two.

It	With	Kith	Lithe
Slick	Pithy	Without	Within
Elf	Self	Help	Helping
Elm	Helm	Hello	Tell
The	Other	Another	Others

The shelf elf is not the same anymore.

She loves to play the same game all day.

Does she want fame? Does she want to make a name for herself?

The name of the game is helping others.

She does not want to admit that she may be sick.

She wants to be at the helm.

She does not want another to be on top.

She must be at the top at all costs.

Ink	Pink	Link	Think

The tall lady loves pink.

She thinks it is a link to her past.

In	Pin	Kin	Link
Miss	Hiss	Piss	Kiss
Ass	Lass	Pass	Mass

Miss Pink does not like to make a mess.

She has one pet that can sure hiss, and another she kisses from morn till night.

She does think that her pets are a link to her past.

One pet wears a bright pink pair of cuff links. Can you see?

The pink-loving lass loves to sit on the grass.

She makes sweet-sounding noises all day long.

This lady will never miss her park visits for the world.

As long as she has her pets in tow.

Ever	Never	Clever	Sever
-ing	Thing	King	Wing

She will never miss it for anything.

She thinks her pet is sweet. That kingly bat that has tremendous wings, you see!

Bag	Rag	Gag	Lag
Brag	Brat	Brash	Brand
Bound	Found	Round	Sound
Aid	Said	Laid	Maid

He found a mandolin in a bag.

He did brag about it.

He was brash.

As a gag he said aloud, “Who laid this brand new bag in the sand? Was he or she sound? I can make a brand new sound on this mandolin.”

Cruel	Gruel	Drench	French
Bout	About	Around	Astound
Pack	Sack	Rack	Wacky
Mack	Lack	Clack	Track

He packs his sacks full of racks of meat.

A wacky guy in yellow slacks.

Clack, clack, he goes on the tracks.

He lacks nothing, nothing at all.

Lass	Class	Glass	Bill Blass
John	Johnny	Jim	Jimmy

Bill Glass is in John's class

He lives in a glass hut, all alone.

The cruel brat drenched his French maid in gruel. He bragged about it too.

The two got in a bout and the brat was astounded at his loss.

Out	Bout	Gout	Rout
Pout	Tout	Lout	Doubt
-ter	After	Matter	Latter
Hind	Behind	Mind	Find

After the bout the brat was bound up.

The maid put the matter behind her.

She wanted to find another job but she was a lout, a lazy gal.

She pouted as she played the mandolin.

She had found her role in life, which was to be a mermaid, not a land-maid.

Main	Pain	Gain	Rain
Worry	Sorry	Lorry	Glory
All	Way	Ways	Always
Again	Away	Anyway	Rainy

The main worry was that she was always in pain. She was sorry about her bout with the lad. She got him a toy lorry. That was glory for him. Glory on a rainy day, but never again, she said.

Age	Sage	Wage	Rage
Know	Knot	Knowing	Knowledge
Tie	Lie	Tied	Lied
Life	Wife	Strife	Knife

The sage does not worry about his age.

He does not know how to feel rage.

He does not have a wage. He does not tie himself in knots. He seeks knowledge. That is his calling in life. He does know strife but he knows how to get his food for the day. Having a computer helps. So does knowledge of the world wide web and what people need today. The sage may live apart from others but knows how to connect with them.

-ty	City	Pity	Witty
Ability	Capability	Witty	Security
Main	Lain	Cain	Pain
Monday	Month	Money	Monopoly

Kimura's ability is known in the city.

He knows how to maintain security.

He has a stare to freeze a giant.

He has been known to lie in bed for months.

He plays with a friend, the one called Cain, a slender chap who loves to cook. The two of them are witty and can go batty and catty for weeks on end. They love honey and baloney because they have no money.

Battle	Prattle	Cattle	Saddle
Talk	Walk	Chalk	Balk
Ask	Bask	Task	Cask
Hide	Ride	Side	Wide
Lose	Choose	Booze	Moose

Junko won the battle of the prattle.

She talked all day and walked all month.

She balked when she was asked to sit on the saddle on the cow. She hid in a cask. She did not think she could ride that day. It would be a battle and a pain to ride and she did not know how to lose. If it had been a moose rather than a cow, Junko would have had the time of her life. If she had her way, she would never choose to lose.

Hood	Wood	Mood	Food
Brood	Room	Groom	Vroom
Leave	Heave	Weave	Here
Rum	Mum	Sum	Bum

In this hood we have wood for food.

In this room we brood with the groom.

In this mood – let us leave the hood.

We cannot weave a life here.

We can only heave wood in our hood.

We do not want to be hoodlums when we can do sums.

We do not want to drink cider and soda when we can do the rumba.

Who wants to be a bum?

How can you face your mom?

Age	Page	Ravage	Savage
Cabbage	Yardage	Usage	Wattage
High	Nigh	Sigh	Thigh
Time	Mime	Dime	Lime

The sage did not ravage the land.

He only ate the cabbage.

He pointed to the dead light bulbs.

I sighed, “What wattage and advantage!”

I got a dime, you know.

I got a lime, he mimed.

It’s well-nigh time to go; it’s night and there is no light.

Night	Sight	Light	Fight
Bight	Might	Right	Wight
Quite	Real	Really	See
Fee	Wee	Bee	Tee
Feeble	Beetle	Wheedle	Peek

It was quite a sight.

A wight at the bight.

It was night all right.

I really could not see.

I paid a little fee.

A wee little fee.

It fit to a tee.

I could really see.

Circle	Cerebral	Cell	Centre

The brown-eyed girl stood in the centre looking very cerebral in her long polka-dot dress. Every cell in her body was taut. As she stepped in the circle she knew that she was going to win the annual maids' dance in Akihabara.

Germ	Gentle	Germany	Gestate
Fortunate	Harm	Barmy	Farm

In a land beyond the barmy farm lives a gentle germ that gestates over many years and only gently harms those unfortunate enough to serve as hosts.

Then	Than	There	This
More	Sore	Bore	Lore
Mean	Bean	Lean	Clean

It was more than lore. The law was on our side.

We were sore there at the park in Halifax but this was no boring picnic.

It was fun and then some.

-ture	Nature	Caricature	Future
Suture	Torture	Vulture	Rapture
Overture	Lecture	Texture	Venture

Sometimes nature is rapture.

Not the caricature of nature.

Like a vulture in a suit.

That is torture to see.

When you venture into the heart of nature.

You will see the texture of greatness, and see the future that we have to protect.

Hoo-	Hoot	Hoop	Hook
Yahoo	Boot	Coop	Cook
Took	Soot	Loop	Rook
Went	Vent	Sent	Rent
Neck	Peck	Deck	Check

After playing a video game, I took my boots and went to the coop. I saw a rook at the vent. I took a hoop and made a loop. The rook was not a spook at all; it was a vulture. It pecked at my neck. I hit the deck; I checked my boots. They were gone and so was the rook, the vulture, I mean.

Chap	Chop	Chip	Chin
Choose	Chew	Check	Chapatti

The chap chewed the chapatti furiously.

His chin went up and down; he chopped up chips and checked his pulse!

Mo	Lo	To	Ho
Ral	Cal	Tal	Tel
Moral	Local	Total	Hotel
For	Nile	California	Talisman
Ought	Bought	Thought	Sought

You ought to visit California, and see the redwood forest. Even in total darkness, you can feel the power of nature. The locals like to camp there and tourists come from far and near. I bought a hotel there once and thought it was quite splendid. The redwood forest, that is. The hotel? I would rather forget.

Act	Pact	Fact	In fact
-tion	Faction	Situation	Condition

You have to act right.

When you make a pact.

Check the situation.

Know the condition.

In fact, know the factions involved.

Then do the right thing.

Split	Spleen	Splay	Splendid

After the spleen of the chicken was splayed on the board the vet exclaimed, "Splendid!"

Spry	Spray	Sprocket	Sprawl

The spry old lady sprayed something on the sprocket. She felt that this was her way of preventing urban sprawl but no one could make sense of what she had done.

Of	-fer	Offer	Buffer
Suf-	-fer	Suffer	Proffer
Deed	Weed	Feed	Creed

What do you have to offer?

Do you proffer deeds or creeds you do not really believe in?

Do not suffer heartburn if you have nothing, nothing truly to give.

Feed yourself and yours, and go your way in peace.

You have done a good deed.

No one can deny that.

Pro-	Prolong	Produce	Proclaim
Protect	Promote	Procure	Serve

The cops are there to serve and protect.

That is what they all proclaim.

They claim to care about all, and will do their best to procure the funds they need.

Cook	Hook	Took	Spook
Ghost	Ghastly	Sight	Night
Rookie	Cookie	Goodie	Kitchen

The cook was spooked when the rookie ghost took the book off his hands.

It was a ghastly sight that night but there were no goodies in the kitchen.

The ghost did not linger to mount a search for cookies and other goodies in the spooked cook's pantry.

Lay	Cay	Say	Way
Gain	Pain	Main	Rain
Delay	Decay	Gainsay	Waylay
Hood	Stood	Food	Wood

I lay there on the cay; they all went their way.

I stood without delay; I did not want to decay.

I stood in the rain, a hood on my head.

The pain I can't gainsay.

Clue	Blue	Flue	Clueless
Crew	Crew-cut	Drew	Slew
Down	Frown	Brown	Crown

We do not have a clue how blue the crew is.

We are clueless in our crew cuts.

Let us check the flue in case the glue is coming down.

I see something brown, quite like a crown.

Do not frown at me. I am down in the flue.

Ire	Tire	Fire	Hire
Sire	Wire	Mire	Dire
Strait	Straits	Wait	Gait

The people stoked my ire, when they threw the tire into the fire.

After I had refused to hire them.

They got me mired in mud.

Reed	Greed	Agree
-ment	Agreement	Disagreement
Dan	Dance	Prance
Very	Every	Everyone

Some say the king is greedy. Some say the queen is kind. Some say the prince is everything you do not want to be.

*Chef	Chic	Charmaine	Chamois

*ch pronounced as "sh"

Charmaine, the chef, in her chamois, looked very chic.

Ear	Hear	Year	Gear

Do you hear the creaking of the gear?

Do you have your ears open?

What a year that awaits you.

Mark	Park	Dark	Stark
Start	Star	Starlet	Admire
Admiring	Hiring	Wiring	Tiring

You made your mark on the field that night. It was stark but you made a good start toward your dreams. You are now a star and you are going to help others reach their goals.

Scan	Scarab	Scatter	Scamper
Brain	Train	Drain	Strain

Professor Nakamura scanned the field for scarabs.

He really wanted to find these beetles and had set up a tent on the field for days.

The good professor was under a lot of strain as he had to supervise so many students.

He drained his coffee cup soon enough and looked as scatter-brained as ever.

Gin	Ginger	Ginseng	Gingerbread
Stay	Stray	Straight	Strict

The Gingerbread man loves to drink ginseng for good health but stays away from gin. He is very strict with himself because he does not want to stray from the straight and narrow.

Drive	Bribe	Scribe
Brown	Black	Blight
Bleak	Blow	Brought
Work	World	Worse

A black and brown car he drives.

He calls himself a scribe.

He says he hates bribes.

It makes the world bleak.

He does love his work.

Things could be worse.

Life could have been a blight.

Scramble	Scribe	Scrabble	Scroll
Scribble	Scrimmage	Screw	Screwball

An ancient scribe scribbled on a scroll what looked like a scrabble game and today we scramble to play it as if it belongs in our time.

Our	Sour	Dour	Hour

This is our day.

It may be dour and sour, but it is ours.

With many hours ahead, we might as well make the most of it.

-able	Billable	Comfortable	Sellable

Is it billable?

That's what the fine lawyers ask.

Because they are bred for comfort, be prepared to pay big bucks.

Street	Stray	Stream	Stroll

We strolled on the street from day to day.

We saw the stream, the creek, the brook converge.

We did not stray far from water.

We felt fully at home on the plains.

Ream	Cream	Dream	Freak
Dress	Dredge	Dread	Dribble

There is a ream of paper in the cream.

What a dream for a freak.

Re-	Act	React	Replay
Movie	See	Fee	Bee

How do you react when you see a replay of your favorite movie?

Or see a bee eating beans?

Fee	Wee	See	Lee
Spree	Said	Sounds	Paid
Once	Twice	Shopping	Mister

"What is your fee?" asked Mister Lee.

"Let me see. My fee is just a wee little bit," I said.

"Sounds good to me," he said, and then he paid at once. I then went on a shopping spree!

Danger	Wager	Teenager	Made

The teenager was in danger when he made a wager.

Girl	Bird	Firm	First
Member	Members	Shop	Shock

Members of the firm first called the girl a J-bird. She shocked them when she said, "No, I am a K-bird." K is for kinetic; "bird" means "I can fly!"

Life	Wife	Strife	One

Strive to live an honest life. It may not be easy, but it's certainly worth trying.

Bar	Car	Tar	Mar
Par	Char	Harp	Harm
Pain	Paint	Painted	Play

The car is painted with tar. It looks charred, but it runs pretty well.

We are on a par; we both play the harp.

Rub	Snub	Nub	Pub

There is the rub. He is such a snub when at the pub; that is the nub.

Look	Cool	Pool	Spool

Glover looks pretty cool in the pool.

He swims with a spool on his back.

Go, Glover! Go, Glover! Keep on swimming like a whale.

Ring	Bring	Sing	Wing
Let	Bet	Set	Wet
Plan	Plane	Wan	Wane

Bring me the ring and let us sing on the wing of the plane. Let us do that before the light wanes. It's pretty dangerous flying blind.

Mean	Lean	Wean	Bean
Robot	Machine	Pretty	Soon

This robot is a lean, mean machine.

It runs on beans, fuel made of beans.

Ash	Cash	Bash	Sash
Color	Much	Such	Lush

With so much cash we can have a bash.

We will put on our ash-colored sashes and whirl around until we are dizzy with delight.

Lousy	Mousy	Bouncy	Drowsy

I may be feeling mousy in this lousy moment. By noon I will be bouncy and no longer drowsy.

Mild	Wild	Child	Blind
Boss	Toss	Loss	Moss
Use	Used	-ible	possible

That wild child is a thespian. She used to be mild. When she is uncomfortable she is impossible. She likes tossing and turning in the moss. What a loss that she is no longer the boss of her own show. She certainly is not blind to her current plight.

Frugal	Brutal	Bruce	Brute

Bruce is frugal and brutal. He is a brute when he wields the baseball bat.

Jay	Way	Say	Nay
Fee	See	Ride	Decide

Jay's Hope

Jay was hoping that he could have coffee with Hina. He did not want to call it a date but Hina decided that she would not go for coffee if she and Jay were not on a date. To settle the matter they decided to walk around and talk about whether they were on a date. While thinking of something clever to say to Hina, Jay fell down and broke his ankle. Hina called the ambulance and Jay was taken away.

Unit	Union	Uniform	Unify
University	Universal	Unifying	Unity
Unicorn	Solution	Global	Warming

Unity and Problem Solving

In this unit we consider the matter of unity in the world. There are many problems that could be solved if we got together as members of the human race to honestly seek solutions. Take global warming, for example. Some universities have been studying this problem for years but there is still no consensus as to whether global warming is the result of human activity. What a farce!

Rain, Rain, Go Away

Nakata and his friends were playing out in the field one day and really enjoying themselves. One of their friends had just received a brand new mini-car from his parents. He allowed all the kids to take turns riding in it. Just when it was Nakata's turn, it began to rain. He stopped the car and raised his eyes to the heavens. His friends looked at him in surprise. He slowly raised his hands and shouted, "Rain, rain, go away!" Instantly, the rain stopped. The other children begged him to teach them the secret of his ability to command the rain. "Just believe, just believe," Nakata said.

Alhambra's Hat

Alhambra liked to wear a bright yellow hat. It made him stand out among his peers and so he was very much attached to it. One day, as he was walking home from school, someone took the hat off his head and ran off. Alhambra gave chase but his little feet were no match for the person who had snatched the prized little hat from his head. One day, on his way from school, he saw a little old lady wearing a hat just like his. He had seen the old woman before and she had never had a hat on. Alhambra decided that he would snatch his hat off the old woman's head. As he did so, the woman's head almost came off because she had glued the bright yellow hat on!

A Fool and His Money

Young Nam liked to play pachinko. He often lost money playing at his favorite parlor but it was so much fun that he did not worry about the money that he lost. He did not have a lot of money to play with so he only lost small amounts. One day, his luck changed. He got on a winning streak. As he continued to win a small crowd gathered behind him. One of the people decided to put himself in Young Nam's service, collecting all the winnings and putting them in a bag. Just before closing time, Young Nam looked back to see that there was no one. All the money and the prizes he had won were gone. Gone with the wind.

Listening

Listening is a very important skill. Even though it seems like one of the easiest things to do there are indications that many people do not listen well: The student who cannot recall what the teacher had said a moment ago, the employee who promptly forgot what the boss had asked him to do, and the father who does not remember what his daughter had asked him to buy for her birthday. Listening requires being mentally present, really focusing on what the other party is saying, and turning the matter over in the mind. If one does not focus intently on the material, it is hardly surprising that it is soon forgotten.

Buyer Beware

When you want to buy something and the seller asks you to make an offer it is very difficult to decide whether to go in very low. You want a good price, of course, but you also want to be fair. Thus, when asked to make an offer you do not want to come across as a cheat so rather than quoting a price that is too low, you quote something higher than what the seller might have expected. That then provides an opportunity for the seller to make a bit of a killing, feigning surprise and asking for a little more. The seller extols the benefits of the product and makes you feel guilty for pushing the price down so low. You end up paying quite a bit of money for something that might not be worth so much. Buyer beware!

Starting the Day

How do you start the day? Do you jump up from bed, head to the bathroom for a brisk shower and head out? Or do you linger in bed for hours cursing yourself for yet another day? If you are not excited about what you do it is unlikely that you will have the energy you need to carry you through a successful day. When you go about your day devoid of passion, others will pick up on it. Few people like misery for company. If you want to make the most of every day find something you love to do and give it your all. If you cannot find the thing that you truly love then you better love the thing that you must do to make a living. Who knows? It might turn out to be the thing that you absolutely love to do!

In the Beginning

In the beginning there was just coffee…and tea. Either of these two words was all that you needed to say if you wanted a beverage and you were sure to get a hot steaming cup of your favorite beverage. These days, we have an embarrassment of riches. You cannot just say you want coffee or tea and wait for a steaming cup of the good stuff. You have to specify what kind you want and there is a profusion of names that are hardly familiar to the average coffee or tea drinker. Some people just look at the menu board and point to something, anything just to get something to drink as quickly as possible. What a terrible waste. Here lies an opportunity to gain an education in the brewing of coffee and tea and join the ranks of the idle rich who always know exactly what kind of cuppa they need and want!

Control Yourself

Whether on the playing field in school or on the streets, there are always opportunities for bullies to pick on one person or another. When you are picked on it is easy to cower in fear especially if you pride yourself on being a peaceful person. You may not want to challenge the bully because of fear for your own safety or in some cases because you do not want to hurt the other person. Whatever the reason might be, it is never a good idea to enter into a fight too quickly. The fight may come to you no matter how hard you try to keep yourself away. This is not to say, however, that you should never be ready to defend yourself. Control yourself but be prepared to defend yourself if need be. This might be as simple as calling the cops rather than walloping the other guy yourself.

What Do You Demand of Yourself?

There is a saying that life gives a person whatever the person asks. If you ask life for the best, life will give you the best. If you ask life for the mediocre, life will gladly give it to you. What do you deserve in life? Think about this carefully before you make any demands of life. Also, understand that there is no free lunch and that the more you demand of life the more you have to give. This does not necessarily mean trading your brawn for what you want unless of course you are a boxer or a professional fighter. You might simply have to work smart and make smart choices in order to get from life what you demand of it.

Theodore Roethke's *My Papa's Waltz:*

A Happy Memory of a Father's Imperfect Love

- By Everett Ofori (California State University, Dominguez-Hills, Humanities Program)

It is virtually impossible to pick up the daily newspaper in any large city and not come across cases of abuse of children, whether beatings, abandonment and neglect, or even murder. In such an environment when our senses might be heightened to the issue of family abuse, it is little wonder that some see in Theodore Roethke's lyrical poem, "My Papa's Waltz," an unfortunate case of abuse, in which the mother, who could perhaps have saved the child, remains silent, and thus complicit in the child's terrible mishandling by his father. Another element that adds a touch of verity to the reading of abuse in the poem is the presence of alcohol, which, once again, numerous stories from Alcoholics Anonymous, the newspapers, television, and radio, see almost as a poison that invariably leads people astray. Readers who see touches of abuse in the poem, however, can be forgiven for their 21st century antennas for abuse, for, while acknowledging that the poem takes the poem's speaker and readers on a wild ride, the emphasis should be on the ride, the dance, the waltz, as it expresses a father's awkward attempt to show his feelings of love for his son.

"My Papa's Waltz" is a four-stanza quatrain. This is an assurance of solidity, signifying that the speaker is speaking from a place of confidence and is not wobbly, emotionally or otherwise. Rather, in this reminiscence, the speaker begins by confronting the truth that the whiskey on the father's breath "Could make a small boy dizzy" (line 2). But does he say that the whiskey makes him dizzy? No! Rather, the speaker portrays himself as being up to the adventure, or misadventure, of the night. Many a man who goes drinking might not come home, or worse, end up in a ditch somewhere. But, in this case, the boy appears to welcome the challenge of waltzing with his father. After all, what kind of child would he be if he gave up or tried to break away from his father's embrace, simply because "Such waltzing was not easy" (line 4). Also, when the speaker uses the simile, "But I hung on like death," some are apt to jump to the conclusion that this was a deadly experience for the child. The truth, however, is that when a child is on a roller coaster, for example, he or she might hang on like death, at once terrified and elated for having the opportunity to do something truly exciting.

It is also no accident that the title of the poem includes the two key words "papa" and "waltz." Papa is an affectionate term that signals a closer relationship than if one, for instance, used "father." In the second stanza, the speaker cements his determination to go the distance with his father. "We romped until the pans / Slid from the kitchen shelf" Lines 5 & 6). It must be noted that the word "romp" points to rough and energetic play, something that fits the stereotype of boys, especially in the 20th century, at a time that might be assigned to the speaker of the poem. The notion that the dance continued to the point where pans were sliding from the kitchen shelf suggests that the dancing continued in different parts of the house, perhaps, starting at the living room and letting the movements of the waltz take them to whichever part of the house the dance led them. The fact that the pans "slide" rather than perhaps "tumble" also suggests that despite the father's inebriation and lack of perfection in executing the waltz, even the kitchen pans certainly approve of this father-son dance! After all, despite the father's drunken state, we see in his rough attempts at dancing a willingness to spend time with his son, a far better thing to do than for the father to have made the pub his second home. It is clear that the mother has seen this kind of wild antics before. She has often had to watch with bemusement as her husband tried to do something crazy but endearing. Thus, "My mother's countenance / Could not unfrown itself" (lines 7 & 8), though reflecting a measure of concern, does not rise to level of panic or fear that the father is going to hurt the child.

In the third stanza, we get a bit more insight into the father's life, and rather than judging him as a no-good drunkard, the reader surmises that he has had a tough life. He has perhaps had to fight and stand up for himself. A hand "that is battered on one knuckle" (line 10) has probably been in fights. But, the father probably does not want that kind of life for his son. Rather, he wishes for a more joyous life for his son. Unfortunately, he is not in his current state the best teacher of waltz for the poor child, as "At every step you missed / My right ear scraped a buckle" (lines 11 & 12). Another unfortunate but bearable memory is found in the last stanza, which says that, "You beat time on my head / With a palm caked hard by dirt" (lines 13 & 14). The child gamely bears these uncomfortable moments interspersed throughout the dance because at heart, he knows the father wants him to have fun, and that, the father is a hard worker, who probably does not see much fun in his life in his efforts to take care of the family.

For those who see this poem as a matter of abuse, the last two lines, "Then waltzed me off to bed / Still clinging to your shirt" should dispel any such notions. For in that moment when the two have covered every ground in the house, eking out moment after moment of joy from what might be a boring everyday life, the bond between father and son is captured in the father's final recognition that it is time to put his beloved son to bed, and the son, for his part, still holding on to the father he loves even while slumber fills his eyes.

It would be disingenuous to suggest that the Roethke's "My Papa's Waltz," does not carry any hint of danger. As Bobby Fong writes in the article, "Roethke's 'My Papa's Waltz,"

> The poem is like a seesaw, where the elements of joy (the figure of the waltz, the playful rhymes, the rhythm), are balanced against the elements of fear (predominantly the effects of dictions such as whiskey, dizzy, death, unfrown, battered, knuckle, scraped, buckle, beat, had, dirt, clinging). The ambivalence of feeling extends to the narrative stance of the speaker. As a student recently noted, the speaker is remembering an incident of childhood, and if the child shared in the father's joy, the adults has learned to understand the mother's disapproval, for the adult stands with the mother, observing.[3]

Not every poem can be read through an autobiographical lens. Even so, an understanding of Roethke's life and background suggests that there might be hints of the author's own life and experience in "My Papa's Waltz." He was born in Saginaw, Michigan, and by the age of 15, not only had his uncle committed suicide, but also his father had died of cancer. It is not surprising that memories of his childhood, even if seen through rose-colored glasses, should remain with him long into his adult life. As Forster notes, "Roethke's poetry reveals much about the poet himself. His poems are often explorations of his own psyche, using imagery from his childhood to describe his interior life."[4] It must also be noted that, unlike today, when children are supervised at the playgrounds for fear of kidnappers and stranger danger, there was a time, when young boys climbed trees, got bruised, run to the nearby creek, fought with other boys, went hiking for hours on end, and that these were all seen as a natural part of growing up. The few scrapes and scratches that the speaker sustains in the embrace of love in the family's kitchen is nothing compared to what a band of boys seeking adventure together might have experienced on their own. Mothers of that bygone era might indeed have expressed their characteristic frown, but they knew deep within that, boys had to be boys, and that boys needed their fathers. In "Roethke's My Papa's Waltz," Ronald Janssen speaks of "an angry mother and a desperate child."[5] A frown is not necessarily always the expression of anger; it can even be a signal of disapproval to be sure. But, when context, time, and place are considered *in toto*, who knows but that inwardly, the mother might have been happy that this bumbling, whiskey-swigging father, knew enough to come back to his family and to extend a

---

[3] Bobby Fong. "Roethke's 'My Papa's Waltz.' *College Literature*, vol. 17 issue 1 (Feb 90), p. 78.
[4] Matt Forster. "Chapter One: Background & Early Life." *Theodore Roethke* (2005):1. Great Neck Publishing.
[5] Ronald R. Janssen. "Roethke's `My Papa's Waltz.'" *Explicator, vol.* 44 no. 2 (Winter 1986): p. 44.

loving hand to a young son who adored his father, despite the father's own love affair with the bottle.

The rich details expressed in "My Papa's Waltz" also show that children are attentive, and that they see both the good and the bad, even if they do not openly express their criticism, knowing that they are just children. But these strong childhood impressions might find expression, for good or ill, when the child becomes his or her own person. For example, some children of alcoholics also become alcoholics, while some children of alcoholics use the negative impressions they might have picked up from childhood as an incentive never to touch alcohol.

The hard life of the father expressed in "My Papa's Waltz" if seen as reflecting the reality of the author's father's own life, might have played a part in Roethke's following his dream to become a writer rather than remain in his small town and follow the family business. The father's lack of awareness that in his attempt to give his son a wonderful time through this wild dance the child is getting his ears scraped might also have translated into greater attentiveness in the author's own life. As one of his students reported after Roethke's death, "As a teacher Roethke was someone who, no matter what we said, took it seriously."[6] In effect, both the good and bad aspects of the father's life, from the positive elements of electing to be with his family and attempting to make his boy happy, to the father's lack of awareness of how he was inadvertently hurting the boy, through the father's life as a hard worker in the fields and greenhouses, might have spurred the boy on to become a more attentive, goal-driven young man, who was able to shake off family pressure to go to law school and to choose the life of a poet. When the author is conflated with the speaker of the poem in this way, then, "My Papa's Waltz" becomes a tribute to an imperfect father that is missed by his son, that is, a happy memory of a father's imperfect love rather than a flashback of remembered trauma.

---

[6] Phyllis F. Dorset, Roethke Remembered. *The Sewanee Review*, vol. 113 no. 3, pp. 450..

References

Dorset, Phyllis F. "Roethke Remembered." *The Sewanee Review*, vol. 113 no. 3, pp. 450-457.

Fong, Bobby. "Roethke's 'My Papa's Waltz.' *College Literature*, vol. 17 issue 1 (Feb 90):78.

Forster, Matt. "Chapter One: Background & Early Life." *Theodore Roethke* (2005):1. Great Neck Publishing.

Janssen, Ronald R. "Roethke's `My Papa's Waltz.'" *Explicator*, vol. 44, no. 2 (Winter 1986): 43-44.

Roethke, Theodore. "My Papa's Waltz." *Southern Review*, vol. 36 no 1, p. 126.

About the Author

Everett Ofori holds an MBA from Heriot-Watt University (Scotland, UK) and a Master of Science, Finance, from the College for Financial Planning, Colorado, USA. He teaches Public Speaking, Management, Marketing, and English for Specific Purposes (Business Writing, Medical Writing, Meeting Facilitation, etc.). Everett has helped hundreds of high school and university students around the world to improve their writing and grades. He has also worked extensively with business executives, including those at the C-level.

Accenture	IIJ (Internet Initiative Japan)
Actelion	JVCKenwood
Artner	McKinsey Japan
Asahi Kasei	Michelin Japan
Asahi Soft Drink Research, Moriya	Mitsubishi (Shoji)
Astellas	Moody's
Barclays	National Institute of Land and Infrastructure Management, Tsukuba (NILIM)
Bandai	PriceWaterhouseCoopers (PWC)
Becton Dickinson	Recruit
Chugai/Roche Pharmaceutical	Sekizenkai Nursing School, Soga Hospital, Kanagawa
Disney Japan	Sumisho
ExxonMobil Japan	Sumitomo
Fujitsu	Summit Agro International
Goldman Sachs	Suntory
Gyao	Tokyo International Business College (TIBC)
Hitachi Automotive	Yahoo
Hitachi Design	

www.ingramcontent.com/pod-product-compliance
Lightning Source LLC
Chambersburg PA
CBHW081106080526
44587CB00021B/3468
* 9 7 8 1 8 9 4 2 2 1 0 5 4 *